FINANCIAL FREEDOM

Transform your money mindset in 21 days

KAMRAN NOVIN

BALBOA.PRESS

A DIVISION OF HAY HOUSE

Balboa Press books may be ordered through booksellers or by contacting:

Balboa Press
A Division of Hay House
1663 Liberty Drive
Bloomington, IN 47403
www.balboapress.co.uk
UK TFN: 0800 0148647 (Toll Free inside the UK)
UK Local: (02) 0369 56325 (+44 20 3695 6325 from outside the UK)

Because of the dynamic nature of the Internet, any web addresses or
links contained in this book may have changed since publication and
may no longer be valid. The views expressed in this work are solely those
of the author and do not necessarily reflect the views of the publisher,
and the publisher hereby disclaims any responsibility for them.

The author of this book does not dispense medical advice or prescribe the use
of any technique as a form of treatment for physical, emotional, or medical
problems without the advice of a physician, either directly or indirectly. The
intent of the author is only to offer information of a general nature to help
you in your quest for emotional and spiritual well-being. In the event you use
any of the information in this book for yourself, which is your constitutional
right, the author and the publisher assume no responsibility for your actions.

Any people depicted in stock imagery provided by Getty Images are
models, and such images are being used for illustrative purposes only.
Certain stock imagery © Getty Images.

Print information available on the last page.

ISBN: 978-1-9822-8714-6 (sc)
ISBN: 978-1-9822-8715-3 (e)

Balboa Press rev. date: 04/25/2023

Contents

Acknowledgements

I owe thanks to all the following.

Nicole Caodie who helped me to realize my script with editing and conceptualizing in better shape. Her support made this work accessible to all. She maintained a clear vision till the end and what needed to be done. Her vision and belief was an inspiration and engine to flow.

Fedde Dijkstra who supported me with interior design and cover design. He has been part of my daily process for over six months. He supported me and my work to come to flourishing. A true gardener.

Leonie, my beloved life partner & soulmate who helped me to finalize this book. She has been a huge support ever since we started our relationship. She has also worked as my stringent editor. Time and time again her insightful comments get me closer to the heart of what I was trying to say. Without her loving support this book would not have become a reality.

I am grateful to all those who supported me through life and taught me life and its magic to create a lifestyle that I can recommend to others.

Introduction

When your eyes are open, you will be able to notice things that you were not able to see before!

Hi there. This is Kamran. I am a life artist, coach, chef, author, DJ, timberworker, lover, tantrica, and more. I live a full life in all aspects. I was born in Iran. My father was a bus driver and my mother was a housewife. I live today as a nomad, mostly in Amsterdam and London. I travel most of the year. I have travelled to over 30 countries which is one sixth of the world's map. I keep learning in different aspects and coaching and sharing this wisdom at the same time. I am fascinated by money, sexuality and power. My life today was a dream out of my reach when I was a young adult. Many people around me thought that my dreams were extremely wild. However my life today is quite normal to me.

I had been working on myself for decades. I transformed my life from my young age to where I was. I created the life I wanted. Then I experienced a period of anxiety and depression. I started to remember the practices that I had learned from years of inner work. They woke me up. They woke my soul up. I changed everything once again, a few years later. It was so impressive that people around me started asking me what I did.

So I started to share this wisdom with them as well. I never thought that I was going to write a book about money or coaching. I read many books and participated in many workshops. I spent thousands of hours and a lot of money on learning about myself. A moment of realisation came when my housemates and friends wanted to learn from me. I started to do twenty-one day courses to create habits for my friends and encourage them to live their authentic self. Guess what? It worked. My friends started recommending me to others and I became busy. I started to feel like I wanted to share this with more people and suddenly it boomed! It became too much to individually coach everyone so I decided to write a book.

I got excited and restless to write and finish the book. I realised I couldn't write if I was not aligned, so it took me longer than I expected. It took me 2020 to write a whole book and since then I have been editing. I have also been busy with travelling, creating, loving and going through my life at the same time.

I did my best to find a good balance around the chapters, language and consistency of the book. I decided to keep the language simple and easy to read for everybody at every level of English.

I want to share with you that I started learning English only ten years ago. Personally, I feel it's a huge achievement to write a book in a language that I only started to learn ten years ago.

Today, December 2022, after the last full moon, I have just finished editing the book. It took me a year to write and roughly two years to edit.

This book is a result of organising some of the teachings that I find basic and important. They are a foundation for life, like the foundation in a building. I believe this book is a guideline for people who want to take the leap and break the old paradigm. This is a guide on how to live authentically.

I am humbled and pleased to deliver this information in this new format to you. I believe all this information has been told and written by various teachers and coaches before me. My work was to give it a different taste and curve to reach a new group of people who resonate with this work in this way. I have collected and organised the practices in this book in an order that I think works. It worked for me.

I believe that every single one of us is living on the path and journey that we choose. During our journeys, we might feel happy and successful or disappointed and stressed.

Based on the emotions that we experience, we might change our direction. We might come back and find another path to start with again. Some of us might find branches that are bridges to other realms and journeys. Some of us might stay until we feel completely drained and move on. Some people stay very long on the same journey and feel exhausted. Some might already be enjoying their journey. Wherever we are, this is what we are here to experience.

When you open this book you might be looking for words to inspire you. Or you might want to learn something. I want to admit that words are not experiences. When you experience something it stays with you forever. These words are just reminders. To remind you of the experience that you are in. The reason I wrote this book is to share my experiences and the information that I downloaded from the universe to motivate you to do the work. In other words, I am inviting you to do the work and live happily ever after.

It is not manifesting that makes you happy, but the journey of manifested desire is full of joy and excitement. I wrote a book about money and how to become independent and joyful because it is one of the most important topics at this moment on the planet in my perspective. It is not how much money we earn but it is how we feel about it.

Why do we start businesses?

Is it for fulfilling our manifested desire? To create what I am here on this planet to do? Or is it just vegetating?

With the experiments in this book you will be able to open yourself up to a Source, creator, god or whatever you want to call it. And then through this you will learn how to let yourself relax and trust and receive it. To receive effortlessly. In other words, to experience the flow.

As a result, you learn how to achieve effortlessly. Which absolutely doesn't mean chill and watch Netflix and earn. It means doing something you love doing, and getting paid for it. What is more joyful than for a kid to play and all of life gets sorted in the way that it should be? What if you are still a kid? What if you can play and life gets sorted in the flow by itself? You are able to buy new toys because it's necessary for the game that you are playing and Source makes that happen for you effortlessly. What if everything is provided and you just have to pick what is yours?

Don't you think that the reason for businesses should be to measure your abilities? And the better you get the more reward you will receive? Because you are simply doing the game very well? Don't you think that the reason for business should be to turn the money around? Because money works like energy. It can make things happen.

What if everybody experiences millions of dollars and as they get what they need they pass it to the next person and go on? What if we all can move the money and create things and share those gifts?

This book contains practices that need commitment and discipline. Just reading the book will help you to achieve the minimum. The information is the minimum. If you already were doing some of these practices then you will know the power of them. I have written and organised this information in this particular way to help friends and family who are open to it. I am extremely pleased to be sharing this information with you, my global family, to be more specific and inclusive.

By making yourself aligned and tapped in, you will allow liberated creation to pass through you and become the master of your own universe. It starts with feeling good and practicing how to feel comfortable with feeling good. I wonder if that is your desire? To get addicted to feeling good is to live in the vortex. I am inviting you to create your own reality in co-creation with others and to cruise on it. I met many souls that thrive and fly. I saw many that got anxious and desperate. I believe every single one of us did so too. The question is: are my eyes really open to noticing the things that I am missing all the time?

I have a desire and an eagerness to share this information with you for the purpose of co-creation. I truly believe the more we all know, the better we all live. I encourage you to share this information if you think it's good practice. Lend this book to the next person and let everybody live their true self.

If you don't feel the call, it's because it's not your time yet. Because it's not asked by you. And it is dead annoying to get the answers for questions that you have never asked. Don't bother!

I also want to admit, I have not practised trauma informed coaching or writing in this book. The practices in this book are designed for people who can sustainably stabilise their state of being. I do not recommend or disrecommend this book to anybody who is experiencing or processing trauma in their life at this moment. Perhaps there is another time that would suit you better than now!

How to read this book?

The best way to read this book is to read each chapter one by one and commit to doing the experiments. Some of them might be a bit challenging to do. Challenges will give you the growth that perhaps you want to achieve with this book. I recommend having a mate or accountability buddy to go through the experiments with. It's good if you explain to each other how you feel and discuss the new information together. To go through this journey solo is also fine. I personally went through most of these practices solo.

I recommend reading one chapter per day and practising the experiments. Sometimes it might take a few days to do a specific experiment. During those days, keep writing your goals and gratitude everyday. I heard somewhere that knowing and not doing is the same as not knowing.
I also created a videocourse about this book. You are able to find this on my website if you feel you want to go deeper.

Goals

The most important quality in a successful person is to set clear goals and to manifest them. The very first quality to create financial freedom and to live in abundance. To start we have to know what a goal is and also be able to define what goal is not. To know the difference between a dream and a goal is also very important.

To achieve these goals we simply begin by writing them on a daily basis to emphasise the power of the mind and create the future that you imagine now and to live into it. Writing goals on a daily basis is like activating witchcraft in the universe. The more you write, the more you believe and as a result, the more you create. It might sound simple and it is! In my humble opinion, it is a much needed dedication. It is absolutely incredible when you realise this power and start using it.

To write your goals and start manifesting them is like playing with your own magic wand. Let us remember the story of Aladdin and the magic lamp. The story comes from the story of the 1001 nights. Aladdin started cleaning the lamp. Suddenly, a strange fog filled up the room and a voice said, 'My Master, I am the genie of this lamp'. 'What is your wish?' The universe is your magic lamp and you can call your own genie anytime.

The genie always shows up, because it is you who is the master. In Aladdin's story, he can ask three wishes. The good news is that there is actually no limit.

What is your wish? You ask for an amount of gold and the genie says: yes master. You ask: I want this and the genie says: yes master. You are likely to be conditioned to think 'but this is not possible', and that is true. And you might say wow I can do that and it will happen and that is true too. Whether you have a reason that it will work or not, That is true. Writing goals is the first step into the journey. It's not the only one. And we always start with the first baby step. Since every journey starts with the first step.

So I want you to invite you to write a list of 10 things that you want to have in your life in the next year. Anything that you feel makes your life nicer. A new computer, a new car, a love relationship, anything that might make you happy or excited. Write the first things that come to mind, and it can be anything at this moment.

LIST:

1. ....

2. ....

3. ....

4. ....

5. ....

6. ....

7. ....

8. ....

9. ....

10. ....

WHY ARE GOALS SO IMPORTANT?

Goals are fundamental. Imagine that you are on a ship in the ocean. Without a destination, you will be lost. Most people follow their social values.

To go to study, find a job, marry, have kids, help them to grow to follow the same protocol. And I want to invite you to look at this beautiful opportunity as life to live freely and dangerously and create a unique lifestyle that suits you the best. On the other hand, I have no problem with the old rat race if you wish for it. It is absolutely bizarre if we don't choose for ourselves, because not choosing is already a choice in itself. If I can choose one time in my life, that time is now.

What would it be?
Would I hesitate?
Would I create a life that I want?

"Twenty years from now you will be more disappointed by the things you didn't do than by the ones you did. So through the bowlines. Sail away from a safe harbor. Catch the trade winds in your sails. Explore. Dream. Discover."

-Mark Twain

The book "What They Don't Teach You In The Harvard Business School" by Mark McCormack tells of a Harvard study conducted between 1979 and 1989. In 1979, the graduates of the MBA program at Harvard were asked, "Have you set clear, written goals for your future and made plans to accomplish them?" It turned out that only 3% of the graduates had written goals and plans.

13% had goals, but they were not in writing. The other 84% had no specific goals at all, aside from getting out of school and enjoying the summer. Ten years later, in 1989, they interviewed the members of that class again. They found that the 13% who had goals but were not in writing were earning on average twice as much as the 84% of students who had no goals at all. But most surprisingly, they found that the 3% of graduates who had clear, written goals when they left Harvard were earning, on average, ten times as much as the other 97% of graduates altogether. The only difference between the groups was the clarity of the goals they had for themselves when they started out.

Writing a goal is quite simple and it needs to activate your brain cells to attract. I learned to write SMART goals and I added an F to it. So it's SMARTF goals that I invite you to write. Every single letter stands for a quality of goal that needs to be considered.

Specific: S stands for specific. Goals need to be specific and clear so for example your goal is a car. You have to specify what kind of car you want. which colour , which model, and everything that you can clarify. The more details you give to a genie, the greater the chance that you attract that exact same thing.

<u>Measurable</u>: M stands for measurable. Every goal needs to be measurable somehow. We can always use an amount of money to measure. Like it cost 100 or 1000 euro for example. or if your goal is a new weight you can say 78 kilograms. There is most of the time a way to measure our goals to make it more clear.

<u>Achievable</u>: A stands for achievable. You have to believe that you can achieve this. It might be something that I don't believe that I can achieve and you think that's achievable and that's totally fine. Most important is to not lie to yourself and you can achieve it. For example, I can't become the president of Brazil. Since I never visited and can't speak the language and actually I can't even enter the selection. And if I write that I want to become the president of Brazil, that's definitely not achievable for me.

<u>Realistic</u>: R stands for realistic. It's fundamental to have realistic goals. So we can not write a goal that I want to have an E.T. Or I want to fly from next year. And maybe you ask why? It is quite simple that your mind doesn't attract things that are not real. And then you might think that the whole process is not working. So let's get real. And the other reason to have R is reasonable. It is important to have a reason for a goal that we have. It makes it more clear and accessible to have reason and act towards it.

Time bound: T is for time bound. Every single goal needs to be time bound. And by that I mean that on this day next year. For the next 3 years I will have this car, mobile phone or anything else in my life. We write our time-bound goals out as if they have already happened. We are literally time traveling into the future where we have already achieved the goal.

Feeling: F is for feeling. It's really important to tap into what you wrote and feel it. I want to invite you to write your feelings in the moment that you have achieved the goal. It is one of the most important criteria that make the goal feel more real and close. These feelings make our brain cells to attract them more and more till they become our reality. In the other words it catalyses the process.

EXPERIMENTS:
- Write a list of 10 goals that you want to have in one year.
- Write 3 things that stop you from achieving your dreams and goals.
- Write 10 **SMARTF** goals
- Follow this example: *Today, the 1st January 2025, I have 500.000 Euros savings in my bank account. I feel proud of myself and confident that I made this happen.*

Gratitude

'Appreciation is higher momentum of alignment with source'

- Abraham Hicks

Today is the second day of finding my authentic-self. One of the most important daily practices is gratitude. The power of gratitude is unknown to many and it is huge. I found out that gratitude is the key to the universe and when we are thankful to the universe, the universe starts to respond. Often we eat, drink and engage in life's activities without dwelling on them, when in fact a lot of time and effort goes into producing such things. Think about how we received food and drink from our mothers and took this for granted. Gratitude is a tiny action but it means a lot. You begin to observe the things that are happening around you and you start to become grateful for them. In other words, when you start to be thankful it is basically starting to communicate with higher consciousness[1] and grabbing attention.

This gratitude practice takes no time at all, just a few minutes a day for such a huge reward, and you might feel more grounded and aligned. You might also feel a lot more energy, and you may even feel some inspiration. Ideally you will experience all of the above combined.

1. Depending on your culture you may call this god

I started to realise that in many religions we can see the same practices. I do believe that some practices in religions are really advanced. In most religions as far as I know, gratitude is part of daily, weekly or monthly rituals; like praying or singing. So, taking a moment to connect with higher consciousness enables us to be thankful and grateful. We can feel blessed that we can breathe, and can experience certain lifestyles. With gratitude, we can acknowledge the belongings that we own in the material world, for example.

I started to write my gratitude in small letters to myself in a daily journal, this would take two to three minutes. For example, I would write in a notebook, 'Today I am grateful for everything in my life'. Now, when I write, there are more and more things to be grateful for, taking me longer and longer as my gratitude becomes bigger and bigger. It is important for me to remember to be grateful for things that were my dreams a year ago or 5 years ago that are now part of my daily life. It is important to me to be grateful for my health and happiness and all the emotions that I experience. On the other hand, it's also really important to be grateful for those things or emotions that I don't really like about my life. By becoming grateful we create space to move on.

Let's say, we are writing our goals. In order to achieve what we asked for, we might experience some difficult emotional or practical states.

This difficulty gives us strength to make ourselves ready and prepare to receive and achieve what we asked for. In other words, those moments that seem difficult, are actually our guides to grow and receive. Therefore, I invite you to observe and recognise those moments as well and be grateful for them.

The best moment to write your goals down is after writing your gratitudes down. This is the moment the doors of the universe are open, and it's the best moment to write these goals. In other religions, as much as I observed, prayers end with requests to God to bring health, peace, harmony and personal requests.

Being grateful and thankful on a daily basis will bring you power and confidence to go out and make things happen in the way you desire. Gratitude makes you aware that what you have is the result of what you did yesterday and called into the universe and what you are doing today will create your tomorrow.

The other side of the coin works like this too. So if you are complaining about things that are happening in your life, surprisingly that also works perfectly and you can attract more of it. It is really important to be aware of exactly where you are, and if you want to move to the next step I invite you to be grateful for where you are now.

Basically the universe always fills you with what you have inside. So if you feel happy, if you feel grateful, if you feel blessed, you will get more of it.

So here's the smack in the face, if you feel miserable, if you feel anxiety, if you feel shit, you are going to get more of that too. This is really confronting, and sometimes even I slip into this pattern. Since we all want to be happy and resourceful we have to feel it. If you just take a short moment to think about your life, there are many things that you can be grateful and thankful for.

Gratitude is appreciation, appreciation is acknowledgement, acknowledgment is humbling. Being humble allows the ego[2] to go into receiving mode, and to be receptive to all those things you asked for. Everyday is a new day, a day to be humble and to appreciate life.

Writing gratitude down is a practice that you have to experience to feel the depth of it. As soon as you feel it, you will fill up and overflow with good sensations. It will become an exercise that you will want to do more often in your life. It is magical and it creates magical momentum for manifestation.

2. The protective part of us

HOW TO WRITE GRATITUDE

Here is my formula for how to write gratitude. It is very simple. I invite you to write every sentence starting with:

I am grateful for....
I am thankful for....
I am blessed with....

For example 'I'm grateful for the sun', or 'I am blessed with the car that I have'. Start writing whatever comes into your head.

EXPERIMENTS:
- Write a list of 10 things that you are grateful for.
- Write a list of 5 things that are not serve you in life.
- Start your day tomorrow by writing your gratitude for ten minutes, allow it to flow freely and follow this with 10 minutes of writing your goals.

Another example of how to write gratitude:
'I am grateful for every breath that I take in. I am thankful for the phone that I have. I am grateful that I can speak English as a second language.

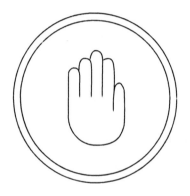

Limits

I grew up in a war. I also grew up in a society where money was a big part of the problem. After the war had finished, the mentality of war and lack of money was dominant in the country. My mother was busy with a demanding business so we had a good flow of money. Therefore we dealt with finances a bit differently to perhaps others who didn't have the same privileges I did. My mother carried a lot of fear around money and poverty nonetheless. I started to have this fear too. It's important to note that the big group of emotions that we experience around money comes from the collective emotions that we experience in our family and environment.

If I live in a neighbourhood where everybody is hassling with finances I will download the same vibes and frequencies as well. Which means that I am going to experience the same worries and feelings. We generally don't want to be the one that will be pointed out as an outsider so we go with what is presented to us. It is really simple how it works. If I see on a daily basis how people do their shopping, what they wear and where they buy their clothes, I am subconsciously going to do the same.

So I start by questioning myself, do I tend to buy food and clothes that last longer or to save money?

Do I empty my pocket as soon as money comes in with the reasoning that I 'need' this? Or do I act through excitement and buy stuff that I like and can use? Do I live in a way that I want? Do I first save or spend? What feels better, a full pocket or an empty one?

Then I begin to consider if I am happy with my shopping, with my groceries and spending. Do I throw food in the trash bin or do I try to finish all my food wisely?

Years ago I discovered that I've been programmed by programs that I watch. The belief systems that my parents taught me. Through years of talking and working with people I heard more of these limiting beliefs:

'You have to work hard for money'
'We don't have enough'
'Rich people are fat'
'Rich peoples are assholes'
'Rich people climb on poor people'
'Rich people are rarely happy'
'Money is an evil'
'I dont have money but god is in my side'
'Money isn't everything'

...and the list goes on.

So if your connection with money is negative yet you are left wanting more, I hate to say it, but that really is not going to work out. Imagine that I tell you that you are not good for me but I want to spend more time with you! Or I want to spend the rest of my life with you, but I have limiting beliefs about who you are. Do you think that is healthy? Does it really work?!

THIS IS A CRAZY CONTRADICTION THAT ACTUALLY HOLDS PEOPLE BACK!

Maybe these thoughts are so deep that I can't even find them, they are buried deep down inside. So to get over this contradiction, the first step is acknowledging the negative feelings towards rich people or money itself. If we want to move forward we have to realise and acknowledge where we are. If we can't see where we are, we will be stuck here until we can recognise it. Feeling is healing, and recognising is the first step.

I would like to invite you to write these limiting beliefs around money down. And start to think and discover where they came from. Where do your beliefs come from and in what way are you conditioned? Do you think rich people are the cause of the problem? Do you think that money causes war?

These are examples you can copy, write them down and find your own. Give yourself space for a few minutes and discover what is happening inside you after reading this. Now, write at least five beliefs you have about money and rich people.

Most kids programs show rich people as evil and there is a poor hero who will beat them. This creates a state of mind that rich people are not good people. But the real question is, is that even true? Are rich people good people? The answer to me is : It doesn't matter if you are rich or not. You can be a good or bad person either way. And what is good to me might not be good to you. It's important to follow our values and start checking what enters into our circle of attention. I meet lots of rich people who do good stuff. I know many wealthy people who are warm, open hearted and help humanity.

On the other side of the coin, often when you are born into a rich family you start to think that money is always there to service you and it will always be there to do just that.

All the belief systems that wealthier families create also set standards and so the new generation are conditioned to attract more. If you are born and grow up in a wealthy family the chances are high that you normally start attracting more money. Lot of rich kids don't even know that they have been programmed that way.

UNDERSTANDING THE PROGRAMMING OF NO!

I notice in our education system and parenting we tell kids NO all the time. We guide our kids with do's and don'ts. So I tell my kid don't touch this. Don't eat this. Don't play in the evenings. We limit them. This same thing happens at school and at kindergarten. As a result we try to follow those rules when we get older.

We don't want to try things that we have been told not to do. We lose our adventurous soul. With money we lose our freedom because we have been told not to take risks. 'You should not gamble', 'Don't buy this or that', 'We can't go to that restaurant'. We actually lose our freedom of choice.

LIMITS CONDITIONING

Fleas are remarkable creatures. They are usually between 1.5 and 3mm long, but they can jump 33 cm horizontally and 18cm straight up into the air. If a flea was a person, this would be the equivalent of jumping straight over the Eiffel Tower, or from one end of Amsterdam Central Station to the other. What is wonderfully amazing about a flea is its physical ability. However if you were to place a flea into a jar with a lid on, it would only jump half the height it has the capacity to. If you were to take the flea back out after a few days, it would continue to jump only to the height that it was conditioned to inside the jar and would never again reach its full jumping ability unless reprogrammed.

And what is even more remarkable is that the offspring of those fleas, even if they aren't kept in a jar, will still only jump to the height of the jar lid. We, as humans, are just as capable of limitation. Think about the things that you don't think you can do because somebody has told you you can't. As small children, we believe we're capable of anything, but usually we begin to limit ourselves. This continues well into adulthood.

When will my nephew, currently five years old, stop believing that it is possible to become an astronaut? I hope, never; but I expect, soon. Not because I will do anything to limit his ambition but because, in the world in which we live, there are so many influences slamming that glass lid down and telling us "that's not possible" or "you can't do that."

I'm here today to tell you that your jar has no lid. If you shoot for the stars you may hit the moon as the famous quote goes but you've got to shoot for something and a lot of people don't even shoot.

REPROGRAM
If I acknowledge that I have been programmed then I can start to reprogram myself. It takes some time to reprogram but is well worth it since our limiting beliefs are deep in our subconsciousness. The good news is that it's possible so let's start by finding out what our programmes are.

What do you think of yourself in your head on a daily basis? **Write this down.**

What do you think of money and what you are capable of? **Write this down.**

Since all these programmes are deep in our subconsciousness the way to change them is to do some kind of surgery. There are many different styles and practices of such surgeries you can do, however the one that I recommend is very simple.

You start by writing a new belief system. First you need to write new beliefs and hang them around your room, kitchen, even the car or somewhere where you can see them randomly. Basically by doing this you are filtering them into your subconsciousness, this is because we can't change them with rational thinking. The only way to change is to create a new belief system. Make sure when writing these new beliefs you are using positive language. Some people would call these affirmation words. Some of these new beliefs may be written like this:

'I am rich'
'I am healthy'
'Money is my friend'

EMPOWERMENT THROUGH SELF-LOVE

One of the fundamental practices to get ready to jump higher is to love oneself. This practice gives you the power to realise where you are and what you are capable of. It is of absolute importance to realise that you are worthy. There is a lot of self sabotage that I want to address in this paragraph and I could write a whole book on this. Yet here is a small practice that I invite you to do.

The first time you look at yourself in the mirror each day, acknowledge your beautiful divine eyes (everybody has beautiful eyes). Tell yourself how much you love yourself. Tap on your own shoulders and tell yourself that you are worthy to live a life that you desire. Do this everyday.

EXPERIMENTS:

- Play nice calming music and write your gratitude for 5 minutes.
- Write 10 **SMARTF** goals for one year's time.
- What is your old belief system? Write at least 5 beliefs that you carry from your childhood. Are you ready to change them?
- Make 5 positive statements and hang them in your house. It's just starting a journey to shift your belief system.
- Stand in front of the mirror. Look at those beautiful eyes. And tell yourself how much you love yourself. Tap on your shoulders and tell yourself that you are worthy to live a life that you desire. Do this for one week. Tapping is really important to embody this process somatically.

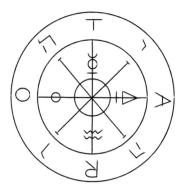

Universal Laws

"The natural laws of this universe are so precise, that we don't have any difficulties building a spaceship and sending people to the moon and we can time the landing by precision of fraction of a second"

- Vikram Sarabhai (father of Indian space research)

When I was studying prosperity and universal laws, I came across a speech that impacted my way of thinking and living. In this chapter I share some of the universal laws that I learned during that period.

INNER CIRCLE

Let us start with an experiment to learn one of them. Write about your inner circle in your life. What I mean by this is write down the people that you are mostly in touch with, this might be your parents, family, friends, colleagues, boss, housemate or your girlfriend and anybody else. Basically I am talking about the 5 people that you spend most of your energetic flow with. What I would suggest is to write down the people who you share your emotions, mentality, attitude and everything in between with. You are learning a lot from them and you have an impact on them too. This is a simple experiment. I invite you to write their names. Next to each of them write their monthly income as well. If you're unsure make a guess or approximation.

Then sum up that number and divide by 5. This is more or less your monthly income. When I heard this for the first time I was like no way! It is crazy! And it is not correct! In fact, through my experiences I now know that this is absolutely correct as I have done this process hundreds of times with many people.

So go ahead and write your name in the middle of a clean piece of paper. Write the 5 people's names in your inner circle around your name. Write their income (maybe just a guess) next to their names. Add these 5 numbers together and divide them by 5. It's crazy, yes!

Now, you might experience that this number is small and you want to change it. The idea is to surround yourself with people that have bigger incomes. Unsurprisingly, these people will provide more of the same energy that attracts abundance. The invitation is to experiment by changing one of the people in your inner circle. This will ultimately change your mindset. So if you think that you have to change them all, the answer is no!

You can start with one out of five. This doesn't mean you will change or forget about the relationship with that person. What it does mean is that it puts you in touch with a person who attracts more financial abundance.

For instance if 5 people around you have 1000, 2000, 1500, 1000 and 500 income, the total sum is 6000. Divide this by 5, you will get 1200. If you have somebody who has 5000 income it will add an extra 1000 theoretically in your income. The invitation is to just give it a try and start spending more time with that new person and you will see the difference.

INFINITY

The other law that I've learned about the universe is the law of infinity and what it means. The important questions to ask here are:

How much food is on planet earth?
How much money is on the planet?
How many opportunities exist on the planet?

Ask yourself did you answer these questions in a limited way or did your mind bring infinite answers? I used to think there was a limited amount of food, money and opportunities in the world. This meant that I had to take as much as I could, because others would take more and I would have less.

By studying the universal laws I realised that there is no limit and everything is infinite. The more we ask, the more we receive and the more we create. Basically money isn't something physical but it's an energy that is shaped into numbers or paper to be exchangeable.

One of the biggest paradigm shifts you can experience is to have a deeper understanding of what's infinite in the universe and how it works.

So, how many stars are in the universe?
How big is the amount of energy source in the universe?
How much food is on planet earth?
Is it enough for all humans and animals?
Can we produce more of it?
Does the planet create more food on a daily basis?
Is there enough space on the planet to make shelter?

I guess you got the idea. How and why does this perspective work? As a person with a limited mindset I will always feel hungry, greedy and dissatisfied. I might feel that if my neighbour wins something, it means that I am losing something. This is a destructive emotion that doesn't help me to create more. It creates war and anger.

I learned that to be able to look forward, in order to create and blossom we have to live in a constructive mindset. An infinite mindset is the way to go. So maybe you think that money is limited and it's not infinite. Let's talk about that.

Back in the time people would farm or have other products that they would exchange. The more you produced the more products you had. There was a time that exchanging one by one was not working anymore and we needed to have a different exchange system. Creating coins was a revolutionary invention. So you could buy and sell freely without using your original product. Our money system has evolved and nowadays it is just numbers in your bank account. What I invite you to look at, is that the more you produce energy the more you will have energy, and this energy can create more energy too. For example, if you're farming apples, your apples are your energy. If you exchange your apples with money, money becomes your energy. Farming apples is connected with you, the earth and the sun which all have infinite sources of energy. So, theoretically you are creating from infinite sources of energy. Therefore your money comes from infinite sources as well.

NO IN THE UNIVERSE

So you may be thinking, 'You know what? I understood the infinity law, I changed the people around me in my inner circle. I am writing my goals on a daily basis. I am thankful for my life and I don't want this lifestyle anymore! I have started saying <u>NO</u> to everything that doesn't serve me anymore'.
Well done! Let's explore further.

One of the big shifts in your behaviour begins by understanding what NO really means in the bigger picture. Basically No is not a No to the universe. When you say 'I don't want this' or 'I don't want that' you are actually giving energy to it. This, in turn, makes it happen again and again. If you don't want things, you have to find out what you do want and focus on that. Let's take the example of - I'm in a pattern of an unhealthy relationship. Instead of fighting with it, which will bring me more of it, I need to find out what kind of relationship is healthy for me and start to manifest that.

WHERE YOUR ATTENTION GOES, THE ENERGY FLOWS

Let's say I attend a protest against something I don't want. By engaging in protesting I am actually giving more attention and energy to what I don't want to happen. So what can we do about this? Support and communicate what you actually want. Use that anger energy to create the reality that you dream of. In other words if you are tired of being broke but you are thinking daily 'I am tired of being broke' you are basically saying no to being poor. Your brain and the universe receive it as 'Oh, this human is focusing on being poor, let's create more of that'. You will therefore receive more poverty. In other words, the universe responds to where your attention is and not to what you are actually saying. Your attention is on something that you don't want and you get more of it!

Imagine that you are a device that is filling up from the source energy and you are receiving more of what you already have inside of you. So if you think that 'I don't want to be poor', you start receiving more poverty. If you think 'I am rich', you receive more of that too. If you can't understand it at the moment it will come by practising. This really does work, I have witnessed this with those I work with. Be who you want to be and you will become.

EXPERIMENTS:
- Play nice and calm music and write your gratitude for 5 minutes.
- Write 10 **SMARTF** goals for one year's time.
- Find out who those 5 people are in your inner circle. Write their incomes and do the maths.
- Formula = (person 1 income + person 2 income + person 3 income +person 4 income + person 5 income) / 5. Change one person in your inner circle and get closer to somebody who has a different amount of income to observe what will happen.
- Observe yourself when you are doing your written or thinking practices. Do you use 'No' or 'I don't want' in these processes? Go over these, rewrite or rethink these and change it into what you want.
- Ask yourself who you really want to be, think about it and write a little bit about that person.

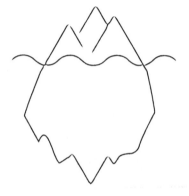

Doubt, Worries & the Subconscious

WHY DON'T PEOPLE WRITE AND SET THEIR GOALS?

Normally we don't write goals because we haven't learnt how to do this. At school we don't learn what a goal is and how to write it. There are many things we don't learn, for example, how to breathe, or about our sexuality, how to dance or what an aura is. Here we just want to focus on goals. Imagine that if you don't know how to play the piano, the odds are really low that you randomly play piano everyday. It's the same with setting goals, especially how to manifest them. The end result of manifesting your goals does not happen from the first day. Therefore, there is no clarity. Perhaps you feel like you're lost in life's river of daily activities. In other words, when you start travelling and you don't know where to go, you might end up anywhere, which can be pleasant or terrible. However, it's nice to flow and at the same time know where the destination is. That's the feeling we are aiming for!

Another reason that we don't write our goals is because we don't grow up in a family and environment where we observe others writing their goals. That is why I found it important to share this wisdom with others to spread the word. So imagine that you grow up in a family where nobody plays chess. Everybody plays football or volleyball. The odds that you become a chess player are really low.

Most likely you will become a football player or volleyball player. As humans we like to do stuff that our parents or other kids in our surroundings do. So we can be socially accepted and recognised. The funny part is that we are automatically goal oriented. As soon as we know clearly what we want, the whole universe starts to illuminate or create the path towards our desires. Basically all we need to know is what we want. The rest you can leave to the universe to provide for us. That's so amazing, isn't it?

Another reason that people are not setting their goals is that they are afraid to fail. As I understand it, we as humans prefer not to do things instead of failing once or twice until we learn. However there is no way to success other than the path of failure. If you are lucky you might succeed in the first try but normally you must fail a few times to learn which way works best. Most geniuses are the ones who are not afraid to fail the most. For most of us, failure is the action you have to learn, which means you have to do it reasonably often. If you are experiencing failure it means that you are in the doing. If you don't experience failure or success it means that you are standing still.

'FALL SEVEN TIMES, RISE EIGHT'
- Chinese Proverb

The other reason we don't do something is because a lot of us are afraid of being rejected. Therefore we don't want to have goals subconsciously. In other words, when others start making fun of me, I quit. Or perhaps I never even start because I am afraid to have a finger pointed at me. A lot of people don't do things simply because they don't wish to be judged. We have to find a way to get beyond other people's opinion of us.

When I was younger and I started to write my goals, people around me started to make fun of me. It was scary, I admit. I have to say it's disappointing to be around people that you love or look up to and they are telling you that what you're doing doesn't work. They think that you have to work hard to get anywhere and that you must stop dreaming. I followed my coaches and wrote my goals. I didn't want to become a billionaire. For me, other things were more important, but they too were out of reach. Today, I have manifested them. Those people who pointed their fingers and judged me, now know that I have achieved my goals. Some of them are proud of me, and some others don't want to acknowledge the reality. Well, what can I do? I believe I have one life and I want to make the most out of it. This following sentence helped me a lot through those times: *'Tomorrow you will regret the things that you haven't done more than the things that you have done.'*

There was a story that helped me to overcome this fear. The story of a farmer who lost his horse. All the neighbours came and said *'Oh, poor guy. You must be so unlucky and we know that it sucks, blablabla',* and the farmer said in return *'Who knows, we will see...'.* A few days later the horse came back with a mare. Now the farmer has two horses. All the neighbours looked at him and said: *'Wow, you are so lucky. It really can't get better than that!'* but the farmer just said, *'Who knows, we will see...'.* A week later when the farmer's son was feeding the horses, the mare kicked him and broke his leg. So again all the neighbours came to the farmer and said: *'Oh poor man he has to do everything himself now, what bad luck has bestowed him, now the work is double!',* but the farmer said once again: *'Who knows, we will see...'.* A few days later, a war started in the country and they wanted all the young men to go join the army. The farmer's son had broken his leg so he could not join all the other young people from the village sent off to fight. Everybody exclaimed to the farmer that he was indeed *'Such a lucky man'* to have his son at home. But again the farmer humbly replied, *'Who knows, we will see...'.*

What we gather from this story is that ultimately the neighbours could only offer the famer their perspective from their own limited understanding!

Nowadays I don't get angry if people say *'No, it can't happen'.* Or they say *'That's a fantasy you're living in'.* For me this no longer gets me down, it motivates me even more. So I say *'Who knows, let's see...'* and my eyes are shining.

The other reason that people don't write goals is because they are afraid to succeed! I understand if you have difficulty understanding this one. We grow up in societies that don't see success and being authentic as a norm. If you follow the norm and become something average it is kind of ok, but many still carry shame and guilt around succeeding. It is also true of successful people, who often have guilt and shame around their achievements. This is such a contradiction because all we want is to achieve a life of freedom and peace and live in it. And quite possibly we feel guilty imagining that life or even living it. The good news is that it is possible to live your authentic self, in freedom and peace and achieve whatever you want in life. You just have to take the time, feel deeply into what you want and how you want to be. This is truly an amazing way of being! To experience a life that is inspiring and marvellous. Freedom and peace are states of mind and they already exist inside of you.

WHAT HAPPENS IF YOU WRITE YOUR GOALS?

I would like to invite you to take a few breaths and tap into the question above.

Choose a goal and sink down into the feeling of this goal.

Personally when I heard about writing goals down for the first time, I was like *'What? Are you serious?!'* Now, today that I am living my goals, the process is in my system and it has become second nature. I know the process by heart and I trust it.

By the way, don't forget that the universe will create an obstacle to check if you are deadly serious. To see if you really want those things that you have asked for. Funny heh! Sometimes they don't even look like obstacles, they might even look like candies or free gifts.

Imagine you decide to travel to find yourself and discover the world, maybe you just broke up with your lover. You have the intention to manifest and plan everything. You buy a ticket, get yourself packed and ready. Just a week before you leave, you meet someone that you recognise the feeling of falling in love with. Maybe doubt arises, huh? *'What shall I do?'* you ask yourself. *'Maybe it's better if I just stay here...'.*
Or it might be that one of your close friends is having a crisis moment and you feel a responsibility to help.

This is the universe creating an obstacle to see how committed you are, to yourself and to self manifestation. I invite you to remember this. This is one of the places where most of us fail.

It's because we forget our goals and purpose and we just want to have fun or be in sorrow. We are drawn in by the lure of emoting with others.

WHERE DO MOST PEOPLE STOP?

Most people stop at 80-90 percent, just before they achieve their goals and missions. Many don't actually recognise or see that they are already 80 percent of the way there. This is because it often looks like you are still in the same place.

I want to share with you a story of one of the biggest gold mines in America from Think and Grow Rich, by Napoleon Hill. It's about two men, Uncle and Darby. Uncle was obsessed with gold mines and he wanted to join the gold mining business. He staked a claim and found an ore of gold. With Darby's help, he borrowed money from all the villagers to buy this gold mine. Everybody invested because they all trusted Darby. Uncle and Darby bought the mine and the machinery. They hired workers and started to dig. At first, it was very successful. It appeared as if there was a huge amount of gold in this mine. However, the further they went, the less gold they were able to mine. The vein of gold started to disappear. It felt like it was over. Finally, with much despair, they gave up and stopped working. Uncle sold the machines and the mine to another man. The new man who bought the mine was really smart and asked an engineer's opinion.

According to the engineer, they would find gold again, very close. Just 3 feet from where Uncle and Darby left off, he found a vein of gold worth millions of dollars. So, they gave up just 3 feet from a fortune!

For Darby, this was the biggest lesson that he learned in life. After this loss, he started to work, selling life insurance. He made millions in life insurance because the lessons of the gold mine never left him. What he learned is that the power of his own mind was more powerful than any gold that he might find. As Napoleon Hill describes in the book, he told himself, *"I stopped three feet from gold, but I will never stop because men say 'no' when I ask them to buy insurance."* Darby owed his '"stickability" to the lesson he learned from his "quit-ability" in the gold mining business.' [3]

This is a skill that I would call boldness. Boldness simply means you keep chasing what you want, with no end in sight. Boldness is a great skill to get a job done. Alternatively, I call it the '10 percent' skill. For everything in life we must expect ten attempts; this is because nine of them might fail. If you are part of the group that chases the ten percent, you will achieve what you want in life. Boldness is not something that you were born with, it's a muscle that you can practice and grow.

3. Hill, Napoleon (2006) Think and Grow Rich. Mind Power Corporation.

THE SUBCONSCIOUS, THE IMAGINATION AND HOW IT WORKS.

Reality is always created twice. Once in your mind and the second time in your real life. Whatever we experience, either healthy or unhealthy, constructive or destructive, happy or sad, it happens first in our minds and then in real life.

I know that there is a huge temptation to say 'you know what, I didn't want this and I have never manifested that'. What is happening here is that consciously you may want tons of money so that you can enjoy life and freedom. This is your desire but it's not what you're experiencing. This is because what you ask the universe is not what you ask with your voice. You ask it with your subconsciousness. Therefore consciously you are asking for a lot of money and deep inside you want freedom. Your subconsciousness however is saying *'money is garbage, money causes drama, money destroys the family'.* This is due to your conditioning or programming.

For example, we may consciously write a goal but subconsciously we emit an emotion. So actually when we say *'You get what you ask for',* what we ask for is exactly what we vibrate on a subconscious level.

It goes even deeper than this. Words have extreme power in them. They create. So we have to be really careful with what we think and with what we say. This also goes for what we listen to, take in and absorb.

The fact is, when you hear someone's words, your inner voice is activated, and your brain cells give an image that represents that word. This then starts to manifest to become reality again and again. For example, if you listen to music where the singer sings 'You broke my heart again and again and again'. This is what you will experience again and again and again. This is because on the subconscious level you have normalised it and started to accept it as if it were the truth. If you listen to the news you start to experience a life full of suffering since the news is full of suffering, hunger and misery.

> *IN OTHER WORDS, YOUR SUBCONSCIOUS*
> *IS YOUR SUPER POWER OF IMAGINATION*
> *THAT YOU HAVE TO LEARN HOW*
> *TO HARNESS AND WORK WITH*

As soon as I learned this, I started to listen to and sing songs that have constructive imagery in them. I started to talk to people who fed my imagination with good thoughts and talked about love and prosperity and the beauties of life. Using your imagination is like accessing one of your super powers on a daily basis. I would like to invite you to close your eyes and take a deep breath and imagine yourself sitting on top of a mountain surrounded by fruit trees. The sun is shining and all the birds are flying and singing. Feel into it.

Take a few minutes to sink into this image.

It's a powerful experience that we can create our reality with our words, with our imagination and basically with our subconsciousness. We will work more on our subconscious and imagination in the following chapters. See this chapter as getting to grips with the foundations and understanding the power of it.

To shift your life in the desired direction, you have to shift your subconscious.

EXPERIMENTS:
- Play nice calming music and write your gratitude for 5 minutes.
- Write 10 **SMARTF** goals for one year's time.
- Observe yourself. If you have worries about your goals, write these down too.
- Write the answers to these questions:
- Have you ever given up before succeeding?
- When was that?
- What happened?
- What would you do differently next time round?
- Write one thing that you want to achieve in life. How could you make ten attempts at this?
- What would you do and who would you be if there was no fear and worry? Describe that person.

Relationship with Money

It's a profound experience to figure out what your relationship with money is like. To understand if you love or hate money. If you have a healthy relationship or an unhealthy one. Imagine that you think mushrooms are disgusting but you want more of them. What is that feeling like? It's good to understand if money serves you or leaves you alone all the time. Think about and answer these following questions:

- Have you always had enough money?
- Do you always have to run after money?
- How do you feel about asking for money?
- Do you normally get paid fairly for the job that you do?
- Do you feel you are underpaid?
- Do you achieve the goals that you write?
- Do you fall short of achieving your goals?
- Do you feel it is unhealthy to have debt?

I realised later in life that I didn't have the capacity to get rich at a younger age. When I was younger I had a high income job and I would spend the money on superficial things. I learned later that I needed the capacity to be wealthy. In the past, I discovered that if I earned more money than I needed, it was easy to spend it all in one go. I would just book a holiday that would cost me double the extra money that I earned.

I prioritised buying really expensive clothes or spending money on superficial items as opposed to things that I really needed to invest in.

If you're curious about how to create more capacity, you have to understand your relationship with money. If you think deeply about what you most desire to achieve in life, that has a direct correlation with your capacity to hold wealth. I would like to invite you to focus now. We will do some profound exercises that have the potential to shift you fundamentally. It does not matter how big or small your desire is.

We grow up in a society where money is seen as an evil that's not good to have a lot of. **Breaking news: that's not true!**

Money is an energy and you can have as much as you have planned for. Just like electricity however, you have to pay a price for it. This is done via physical, mental or emotional work or a combination of all three. The other good news is if you learn how to play smart you can get a lot of money very quickly. If you are underpaid in jobs that you do, you have to redefine your values and relationship with money.

One of the best practices that I ever did in order to change my relationship with money was to write a love letter to money itself!

I would like to invite you to write a love letter to money and express how much you love it. Just imagine that money is your lover, and express wherever you feel it is supporting you in your life. Express in this letter where you feel that it can be more present and where it could support you more in order to achieve your dreams. And if there were times where there was not enough money, say that you can forgive it. Pour those emotions out onto paper. Express if it was used by some people for power play. Express that you know it wasn't the money's fault that it wound up being played in that power play game. This is your chance to write a new relationship between you and money. Express what kind of relationship you imagine that you could've had and would like to have with money. Ask yourself how you can support each other in a healthy way and write it down. How will you support money to be a tool of change instead of a source of shame? Why not describe how you can cooperate to make a beautiful world together, for you and for others. How you can invest this energy for good causes.

ARE YOU READY TO BECOME RICH AND INCREASE YOUR CAPACITY?

Write this letter and just feel all the emotions that you experience. Write them down too. When you write this letter, imagine that there is no other time to fix this relationship but now, and the only way is to be as transparent and honest and direct as possible. Please be fully yourself and don't try to escape. This is fundamental work.

THE RELATIONSHIP BETWEEN CAPACITY AND DESIRE

Our capacity to get rich has a direct correlation to our desires. Most families and communities teach us not to be greedy. It is seen as bad to have more money than others. That it is better to share. What I realised is that the more money I have, the more money I can share. In order to achieve this I must cultivate expansive and inclusive desires, so I can begin to make things happen.

EXPERIMENTS:

- Play calm music and invest five to ten minutes to write your gratitude.
- Write 10 **SMARTF** goals for one year's time.
- Write a love letter to money. Create a ceremonial space. Light a candle. I would like to invite you to take paper money and use it as a representation for the energy of money. Start with being thankful for the places where money has supported you in your life. Write about the moments when you felt you were not supported by money. Write about the moments when you felt that you had no money. Write about how much you love money and what kind of relationship you would like to have with it.

The Stream

I would like to ask you to finish your love letter to money before starting this chapter. The love letter experiment is such fundamental work. Now, once that has been completed it is time to give that money a character. The idea is to find a piece of paper money that will represent the 'money' character that you wrote your love letter to. It can be any note from any currency. Feel into which currency you are most comfortable with. Perhaps it is a ten euro note or a fifty euro note or maybe it is in dollars or peseta. What matters is that you have a relationship to that currency. Now that you found that representative piece of money, it is going to be time to read the letter to it. So, take your time and do that in silence and in a ceremonial space. Light a candle and sage. Make your own altar and then read the love letter out loud, treat it like your lover. The more serious you make it, the more you will profit from it. This will of course not be the one and only time you will get to do this.

After you read the letter, it's time to write one sentence from your love letter directly onto the money. I want you to think of someone that you can share your love with. Someone from your family or friends or perhaps a stranger. The idea is to give this money away to someone as a gift and to explain the experiment to them. To set your love free. This will then come back to you in a more expansive and liberated way.

By completing the last chapter, along with the potent process outlined above of actually giving the money as a gift, you are actively creating the capacity to receive an energetic flow of money.

But wait! Just before you give away the money, I would like to invite you to read the following information carefully:

As we said earlier, Money is energy. Energy has to move.

I want you to embody this message: *the more energy you move the more energy you receive.* By continuing to move this money you create space to keep receiving it. It becomes like a riverbed where water moves through it. There is almost always water in it but you don't know if it's the same water. The fact is, the faster it goes the faster it comes. It is a stream of energy that moves fast. All you have to do is trust and believe yourself that you can work with this cycle of energy and you are a part of it. Actually, this stream of energy is huge, and the cycle is happening all the time, whether you are aware of it or not, just like gravity.

Imagine that you are a vessel to receive and transmit this energetic flow of money. So the more you desire, the more you receive because the whole universe is working to fulfil your dreams. With this theory all you need is to find out what you really want. How it will come to you is not important.

What you need to work on is to create space for the energetic flow of money to arrive. I want to review what we have talked about until now.

First, we wrote our goals which gave us more clarity and a clear direction. We have our safety money which makes us feel safe. Now is the time to feel freedom and love by fulfilling our goals and passing the energy of money to others too. You took a little piece of money and ceremonially spoke to it, writing your sentence on it. Now you can find someone to give that piece of money to. Remember to share the story with them too. If you've done that, let's try another fun experiment!

I would like to invite you to look at your wardrobe and find one of the most precious pieces of clothes that you own. One that you don't wear so often or you haven't worn in the last six months. Think of someone in your life that could make good use of this item. Someone you could make happy by giving it to them.

I practice this often. I give away all the clothes that I haven't used for the last six months and guess what?! There's more space to get new stuff! Normally my wardrobe is full again within just a few days with free stuff! *Crazy, hey!*

You can try it yourself. There is no better day than today to create the reality that you want to live in. It all starts with creating space in your life so that you can receive more.

WORTHINESS

To understand your relationship with money deeper, it is a good time to ask yourself these questions:

- Is it bad to ask for money?
- Can I borrow money?

I discovered that one of the fundamental blockages and limiting beliefs that we experience are around borrowing money or asking for help. This is correlated with worthiness. I want to give you some clarity about this topic. The first question is: which country has the most debt in the world? The second question is: which country is the richest country in the world? The third question is, are rich people happy to borrow more money from banks or others?

Yup, of course the answers to the first and second questions change over time, but the relationship between them stays pretty stable. Here is an example: if the United States has the most debt, it's probably the richest country in the world too. Rich people don't mind asking for money. There is no shame in borrowing money. So going back to the first question, can I borrow money? Yes, of course! Is the answer.

YOU ARE WORTHY OF THE MONEY IF YOU HAVE A PLAN FOR IT

Think about why you might borrow money. Is it to go on holiday? To gamble? Or do you have some constructive plan for it? How long will that plan take you to pay that money back? There is a method if you want to borrow money. We borrow money for constructive plans and we have to know how long it will take us to get the money back. Now, let us look at whom we could possibly ask. Sometimes we have to ask a few friends and make multiple agreements for how we will give the money back. What if they say no? you may ask. Does that mean they don't trust me? That they don't like to lend money? That they don't like me? Are they unsure whether I can pay the money back? First of all, let me clarify something: nothing is personal.

Here is an example of how to understand borrowing money. For my new startup business I need 5000 euros to cover all costs and I already have 3000, but I still need 2000 more Euros. I am dedicated and want to start this business and the only thing that I need is another 2000. I know this new business will give me two hundred euros per month, and I have a backup plan that gives me another few hundred. So, how are we going to get this money?

What I need to do is write 5 to 10 names of people I can ask for support. I will make time to go and meet them in person and tell them all about the plan and tell them exactly what I need. In asking them to lend me some money, I must also state the terms for repaying the loan that work for me, and ask if that suits them as well. If you follow this, and speak clearly, you will be surprised by how quickly you will get the extra 2000 and how little negotiation you need to do.

I would like to invite you to just do it with a small amount now and borrow 100 euros from a few people and pay them back in one week or two. This is a good exercise to make yourself comfortable with borrowing and paying back money. This skill will be a great help for you in climbing the ladder of success.

EXPERIMENTS:

- Play nice calming music and write your gratitude for 5 minutes.
- Write 10 **SMARTF** goals for one year's time.
- Write 1-2 sentences from your love letter on a piece of money. Find the person that you want to share the story and that money with. This initiates the energetic flow of money.
- Check your wardrobe and find one or more items of shoes or clothes that you are willing to give away. Find the person you are going to give this item to. Remember to do this often, every 2-3 months.
- Borrow some money from a few people and make an agreement to give it back to them in one week. Observe your feelings before, during and after. After you pay them back, make sure to write down notes about how this process felt for you.

Having, Doing, Being

WHO ARE YOU ?

Today I want you to begin by thinking about this and writing it down. The invitation is to use all of your intelligence and imagination to explain who you are. So go ahead, grab some paper and have a go. Do take your time with this.

So essentially, I am the total sum of all the experiences I have had. I resolve the emotional equations that are presented to me and based on that I have created a belief system that I live by. From this system many things happen automatically, let's call them habits. So who I am is a result of those habits. These habits are the things that I do on a daily basis.

Ask yourself these questions:
- What are my main habits?
- Can I change my habits?
- Do I have to change my habits?

The most important question to ask yourself is:
- Am I generally happy?

Where we are today is the result of the habits we have now. If I want to have different results I have to change these habits. In other words, who I am now is what I call being.

A new way of being is the result of finding new and different ways of thinking, acting and formulating new habits.It's so important to realise that who I am now is the same as what I am able to manifest at this moment in time. By this I mean, I am a product of my energetic field which is attracting the most of what I am now. We all have habits and beliefs about ourselves, and the reason they are so important is that they control what we have, do and how we act in our lives. So the question is, what can I do to change who I am and as a result create a new me?

Let me explain: imagine that you want to become a doctor and you have just finished your high school. What you now have is a high school diploma. What you want to do is study at university to become a doctor.

Normally if you want to become a doctor, and you <u>have</u> just received your high school diploma you are on the path to becoming a doctor. You still have to <u>do</u> more academic study, finish university and do your junior doctor placement year. Then finally you will be a doctor. This is **having, doing, being.**

Having ⟶ Doing ⟶ Being

Now let us look at a new way of thinking, that you start first from <u>being</u> a doctor, which means you already feel that you are a doctor. What you are going to <u>be</u> from today is a doctor.

Then you have to do everything that a doctor does and you study like a doctor does. Then you will have the doctorate. This is **being, doing, having** - you have swapped the paradigm. This formula applies to everything in life. People and society tell you that you're not anything until you have 'become' something. What I want to offer you is, you already are who you want to become.

Being $\longrightarrow$ Doing $\longrightarrow$ Having

So to clarify, first you must make the time to decide who you want to be. Whatever it is, it actually doesn't matter. The universe doesn't care what you want to be but it does support the effort in becoming. If you want to be a millionaire, a musician, an actor, a naturist or having a big successful company, (whatever it is that your wild imagination gives you the ability to desire) it will support you.

To get a grasp on how this works, first start to find out what your ideal life looks like. Start to write about it. Imagine what that ideal life looks like, feels like, smells like? And furthermore don't just imagine it, let's start acting like you already are this person from today. Literally fake it till you make it, as the age old saying goes. As a result, if you believe in it, you will experience this new being. If you know what you want to do, just act on it. Get emotional about it and feel into it. The more you believe, the more you feel, and the more you feel the more you receive.

If you are thinking you don't know how to make it happen, there is actually no problem. You just need to know what it is you want. The whole universe knows how to make it happen, better than you know yourself. If you have an idea, act on it and don't sit back worrying.

CREATE A NEW LIFESTYLE BY CREATING NEW HABITS

For example, you might want to have freedom in your finances. Perhaps this means that you can buy anything you want in the supermarket. The answer is simple, just do it. Even if you say to yourself 'But I don't have enough money', that's ok, just do it once a month. Go right ahead to the supermarket and buy what you desire. Feel into it. Do not be afraid to buy everything you see because it's expensive. Don't even look at the prices but buy things that you are going to use. Have an appreciation for your body and the products that are going to enter your body. Book a day at the spa and enjoy it fully if that is what financial liberation looks like to you. Don't feel guilty but feel bountiful and enjoy the full spectrum of the experience (the smells, colours, sounds, tastes). Try things out. Learn and feel into who you want to be and what your real desires are!

For me this process is where I learned that I actually want to have a really high quality lifestyle. Surprisingly, it doesn't cost me much. Involve your morals in your new habits. Often when we transform, we get so inspired and excited that we start to tell other people what to do. Be conscious of respecting other people's choices and energetic fields. Our aim is to stay centered in our own being without judging. The more you play this new being the more you will become this new being. So let's get into who this new being is!

I invite you to imagine this new You with all your new habits. Write them all down. Find out what gives you pleasure, write that down and then explore that new persona by being it. Live that character, as if it is you acting in a movie. It is the movie of your life however! You have got the chance to be the change. You have got the chance to make it happen. Trust that everything is going to fall into place. Just be brave and live your best version and best life possible.

EXPERIMENTS:

- Play nice calming music and write your gratitude for 5 minutes.

- Write 10 **SMARTF** goals for one year's time.

- Think about who you want to be and how it looks and feels to be that person. Write about your new being in detail. Write what a day of this new life would look like. What are you going to eat, where and with whom are you going to share the food? What does your house look like, what are the details? Write them down. How do you feel on a daily basis? And who are your friends and what are they like? Check your new bank account and write out your new balance. What kind of car/transport would you have? What kind of activity would you be doing on a daily basis? Get creative and let the imagination flow yet stay realistic.

- Write down a few of your habits. Think about where and when you started doing them. How constructive/ destructive are they? If you want to change these, what are your new habits going to be?

Law of Attraction

When I first got introduced to the Law of Attraction I was like wow! I got super excited. As soon as I started to work with it I felt extremely uncomfortable, because I understood it and I realised I had to change. It was the change that created discomfort.

My invitation to you during this chapter is that if you feel discomfort, stay with it and dive deeper into it. My practice was to listen to the audio of the movie The Secret (a movie primarily focused on the law of attraction) for a couple of months daily, and I started to shift my paradigm.

Let us dive into the law of attraction. It is a simple law that says 'like attracts like'. This means that whatever you vibrate you will receive. We live in an ocean of motion and we just receive the motions that are in harmony with our vibrational body. Or in other words, launch the thought, and the source[4] will join the thought. Then it is possible to unify, blend and suddenly your thought has become your reality. This is constantly happening whether we are conscious of it or not. It is driven by the universal desire to continue becoming. Believe it or not, the non-physical part of yourself (your higher self) knows all of this.

> *WHERE DO I CREATE ALL OF THIS VIBRATION?*
> *IN MY MIND*

4. The Source is the ultimate creation or God as many people refer to it.

Let's get clear on this: every cell, every organ, every part of your body is constantly vibrating. There are high levels of energy happening all the time, even though you cannot see it with your naked eye. If you were to look at your body under a microscope, every cell is made up of electrons and protons and they are moving rapidly. Your brain controls the speed, shape and form of everything that you experience in your body.

The next thing we have to get clear about is that you have a conscious and subconscious mind. Most of the time we access the conscious part of our brain. Your brain ultimately shapes your energy using your subconscious mind. What this means is if you get an idea today you have the capacity to immediately change things towards achieving that idea. But this does not play out necessarily as you may think or expect. You have to understand and work on a deeper level and shift your paradigms to change your habits in order to achieve that idea.

Let us imagine that you grow up in a healthy athletic family. The odds are really high that you will become a healthy and/or athletic person. Because the norms are to be healthy and athletic. As a child you will decide (consciously or unconsciously) to be like them, this then forms the energetic fields which are supported by the activities that you do.

If you don't like your family, or feel different from them, then your subconscious will want to become anything but an athlete. Or perhaps you will want to become more successful than them, becoming the greatest athlete in your family. This can all take place before you really decide or realise that this is happening.

That is how the subconscious works. It creates and shifts all your energy and in doing so shifts our focus. Another example is if you grow up in a family that is rich, you might experience that you live life with a lot of money without knowing why others find it difficult to earn money. Even if your family lost their fortune, you may well make another one easily. Another example of this still applies if you grew up in a family that had to work hard for money. You will feel that you must work hard for money for your entire life.

As I have seen, however, some people complain that the law of attraction doesn't work. And that is absolutely right. What I mean by this is that it works, but not in the way that they imagine. If I write my goals everyday I start to think that I will change my life. Deep in my subconscious I still believe that I have to work hard for money. This old belief is radiating and therefore I still have to work hard for money. This means the law of attraction is not beginning to work in the way I desire, because I am subconsciously ordering something else with my old belief driving it.

So watch out, it's fundamental to change your paradigms! Your paradigms are stronger than your words. They work every second to create the energetic fields that you live in.

> *TO CHANGE YOUR RESULTS, YOU HAVE TO CHANGE YOUR PARADIGMS*

You have to be aware of what is happening in your deeper thoughts. Only then can you make free choices. You can feel that the source is supporting you to become what your thoughts are directing you towards. Basically what I mean is you will become exactly what you are deliberately thinking, every single second of your life.

HOW DO I CHANGE THE PARADIGM?

First of all, we have to agree that the result of what you did yesterday made the life that you have today. To change the result for tomorrow we must change our routine activities. Another thing that we have to agree on is this law of attraction.

> *WHATEVER YOU THINK OF CONSTANTLY ENOUGH WILL BECOME PART OF YOUR SUBCONSCIOUS MIND*

When you give energy to thoughts, when you are feeling them, the whole universe starts to respond and begins to make that happen. Everything is created twice, which we already spoke about; once in our thoughts and the second in the material world. You don't need to know how, but you need to know what it is exactly that you are aiming for. After you know what you want, as soon as you get an idea, grasp it, start to solidify it and it will begin to happen. Be persistent in harnessing these deeper thoughts because the reward for this is huge.

Take time for this following process, which will enable you to start recognising your habits and paradigms. I would like you to imagine yourself from the outside. Give yourself time to do this experiment and get lost in these questions:

- Write down who you are.
- Write down how you see yourself.
- Write about your body and your skills.
- Write about your relationships.
- Write down the self observations and emotions that arise when you're writing the above. This is also a good moment to observe how you are thinking about yourself. Including these will enable you to start seeing your paradigms.
- Now dwell on which habits/paradigms have been making you the way you are.
- Write about everything that you love about yourself and write about everything that makes you happy about yourself.

When I talk with people they often tell me that they are too tired to work and that they don't have enough financial security. That they don't have enough. They have to work hard. I can now easily recognise people's paradigms when we spend time together. Lots of us have been manipulated by a particular paradigm called the 'rat race'. There are many many more of these paradigms like the 'not good enough' paradigm or the 'being an athlete' paradigm.

A lot of work and effort is being expended on these sub-conscious paradigms. In the rat race example we work very hard and then reward ourselves by using shortcuts to enjoyment. We try to buy happiness, perhaps by buying expensive clothes or items. This is often because we don't have enough time to enjoy ourselves. This is exactly what many marketing agencies feed on, to make you believe you need their products to feel good when we actually don't need them. Every season there is always a more expensive toothbrush and more expensive clothes and shoes to buy. Thus we work harder to buy a bigger house or better car just to feel a little bit of happiness. Look at the short term vacation fix, expending so much on so few days, buying stuff that only gives a temporary sensation of satisfaction before joining the race again.

Let me tell you something though, happiness is a state of mind and you can't buy it. There is only one way to access it. To find your authentic-self and live deeply into it, to start tapping into the law of attraction. The best job that you can get paid for is the one that you do with pleasure and that encourages you to continue becoming your authentic self.

QUICK RESULTS

You might tell yourself 'But I am doing the work, give me my results universe! Quick, quick!'. What we must understand is that we need to have time between asking and receiving. It would be horrible to think of something or ask for anything and then it appears. If I think of a rhino or volcano and it starts to happen in my living room, I really don't want that! The time and space between the asking and the receiving is to check that what you asked is something you really want.

HOW TO CHANGE THE PARADIGM?

It is fundamental work to change the paradigm and as a result you will receive a different material world. A different state of mental health. Different emotions on a daily basis. A reality that will surprise you and make you happy in new ways. It's really important to remember that to get the life of your dreams you have to surround yourself with higher consciousness. You have to learn to think differently and stop wanting to have so much control. You have to trust the universe and the vibrational energies.

All you have to do is to create new paradigms and patterns and stay loyal to them. This is a fantastic time to gather all your power. Write who you are and what you believe in. Start watching inspirational speeches and movies. Take your time to nurture and cultivate your new patterns. Imagine that you are the creator, and you're here to create your own life. Write about the house that you want to live in. About the family that you will have. Write about your dream job. The one that you do for satisfaction. Imagine that you have multiple sources of income. Imagine your lover(s), and what an amazing relationship you will have with them. Go deep into the details of your amazing new sex life. Write about anything you want. A nobel prize or a chain of restaurants. Perhaps it's living on the beach you desire and being a coach.

Keep writing these every day! Wake up an hour earlier every day and write everything again and again. Let this become your addiction. It will create a new paradigm in your subconsciousness, and this in turn will attract what you need to achieve your desired life. It will attract all you want to be. I have to reiterate that it does create discomfort however. Remember transition is uncomfortable! When I was listening to the audio of the movie The Secret everyday, my family would mock me: 'But why do you listen to it every day?' and I would say 'If you were to understand it, you would repeat this every day too, over and over'.

This is just the start. You repeat the new information, and the information and energy field start to become one. Slowly you see that you are attracted to different people. This is because you are now attracting people that you are in harmony with. You will also attract the energies that are in harmony with yours. This is the time that you are able to change the paradigm. It's actually very brave to act like this. It is time to start to act like the person you want to become!

Ask yourself the following question:
How much money, bliss and abundance can I receive?

Imagine that you are a vessel like a jug or a ship. Each vessel has a capacity for a quantity, this all depends on where and how you are going to use it and what needs to be done. This includes the amount of money that you can receive. The source (you can imagine it like water that flows into and out of the jug or the wind that drives the sail of the ship) doesn't really count the amount so it is better to think of yourself as being the vessel. You have to understand it's not for you to 'keep' per se, it comes through you, and passes on. The more you tap into and change your paradigms, the more you become your authentic self, growing into a larger vessel and allowing you to pass more on. Then in turn you will start receiving more. If you are in a place where the stream is bigger, you will become a bigger vessel too. To see yourself as a vessel is one part of the paradigm shift.

Let's imagine an example: you are creating a huge company to grow sustainable vegetables in your region. You need X amount of money. This will present certain possibilities and you have to act on them. Now, imagine that you just want to start a small local shop to support your neighbourhood. It's a different quantity of energy required, the local shop compared to the huge company feeding a whole region.

So, to repeat, the law of attraction says 'like attracts like'. You have an energetic field. This energetic field radiates. It radiates based on your subconscious mind. Your habits form your subconscious mind. Therefore, you attract things in life through your habits. To change your habits, you must change your paradigms, then everything will change. It is slow and steady work. It is fundamental work. Commit to it and your reality will change.

EXPERIMENTS:

- Play nice calming music and write your gratitude for 5 minutes.

- Write 10 **SMARTF** goals for one year's time.

- Write down the habits that don't serve you. What can be new habits that will serve you?

- If you had the power to recreate yourself, how would you describe this new person? Write it in as much detail as possible. Include your job, relationships, hobbies, travels, lifestyle and living situation and anything else that you can think of.

- Write who you are. Write down how you see yourself. Give yourself time to do this. Write about your body and write about your skills. Write about your relationships. Remember to observe how you are thinking about yourself and include your emotions. Can you write down which habits/paradigms have been making you the way you are?

- Write what doesn't serve you in this present moment.

- Write about everything that you love about yourself. Write about everything that makes you happy about yourself.

- Come up with 10 things that you don't have and you want to have. Write them in the present tense as if you had them and express your gratitude for them. For instance: 'I am grateful for the multiple sources of income that are continuously supporting me'.

Energy Waves and Clouds

What do we see and what don't we see with our eyes?

We see the things that we want to see. If you sit somewhere and look around, everybody has their own view and perspective. A group of people watching the same movie remember scenes that others haven't. This is also exactly how we live in the material world. We notice the things that we contemplate more often. To look at it deeper we can say we see the things that we believe in. Maybe you are someone who can already perceive energetic fields. Maybe you can feel them, or maybe you can't. Even if you can't right now, everybody has the capacity to perceive these energies.

As we already talked about, our body is energy. When you look at your body with a microscope you can prove this. But there is also another energy that runs through the body. This energy is guided by our belief system. Our paradigms. It is approximately four metres all around you in fact. Like a ball. It has colours, if you are able to see them. This energy has different centres. In eastern cultures it is referred to as the 'chakras'. All the chakras and their unique energies create your own energetic field, which is filled with information about you. When you have people around you this information starts to communicate. That is why we feel comfortable with some people and we don't feel comfortable with others, without really knowing why.

Our energetic field is intelligent. Literally we have antennas, similar to what ants have on their forehead.

Each person's energetic fields are different in their own way but they all work in the same way. They vibrate and they communicate with higher consciousness. By changing our habits and paradigms we change the speed and shape of this energy. All these energies are actually the same, the difference is in how they are shaped. That is why when we manifest something we start to receive that from the universe. This is because the shape of our energy starts to shape the desired reality into becoming.

So now I want you to imagine that you have a new belief: *It's always sunny and nice here and everybody loves each other.*
When you believe in this thought you create a wave of energy. I want you to imagine that most of your neighbours believe the same so they are all creating the same waves. All these waves will attract each other. It's still a simple law: like attracts like. Remember this from our last chapter? By gathering these energies together they become like a cloud. The stronger this cloud is, the faster it becomes materialised, because of this energetic field. It is crucial for the collective to understand what our belief systems are based on. If we all believe the earth is getting destroyed that is what we attract. If we think that we can change our behaviour regarding pollution, we will attract that too.

To understand how energy clouds work it's best to go to the places where there is a strong belief system. Like a church, a temple or Mekka. In those places what people collectively believe works. This is because the cloud of energy is so strong. That is why prayer works. It's basically a way of shifting paradigms by repeating something on a daily basis. The more you give energy into it, the more it becomes real.

WHAT IS AN AURA?

A few years ago I started to feel extreme physical pain. I got sick and I had diarrhoea for a few weeks. I didn't know what was happening. Doctors found no explanation even after doing all kinds of investigations. The only thing that we could agree on was that I was lactose and gluten intolerant all of a sudden. Today my explanation is that I was in a deep depression and my aura was filled with energies that didn't serve me. I had a partner that was not emitting the same energetic field as me. I was studying at university in a field that didn't interest me. I had classmates that I had nothing in common with. I was living in a house and neighbourhood that didn't serve me. I found out later that apparently my neighbours had depression too. My friends and I were relating through victimhood. To be with them I had to lower my frequency, which was not making me happy. I was surrounded by things and people that I had nothing in common with anymore. I was constantly numbing myself to live in this environment.

As a result my energetic and physical body shut down. I lost 20 kilos in two weeks, stopped my studies, and ended my relationship. I lost my financial resources and was forced to change everything. I felt like my world had exploded. This was my energetic field protecting me and realigning me. Deep down inside me I was full of a desire to shine. To become another person. I wanted to be in a different place, to travel and to start work that was purposeful. I wanted to have more meaningful relationships. My life falling apart motivated me to change my paradigm and to start a new lifelong journey of self-discovery.

This story is an example of your aura and how it works. So as we speak there are energetic waves around you. All together they create an energetic field. This energetic field is named an 'aura' in some cultures. Your aura says everything about you. If we could see these auras and translate them, life would become easy. However, although most of us can't see them we can definitely access parts of them. We feel them whenever you feel strange before going somewhere. Or if you feel stressed. Or if you feel happy. These are the signs to know what to do and what not to do. It helps inform us on how to make decisions and could be seen like a navigation system. It also informs our intuition, like having access to your inner guru or inner teacher. I learnt about and practiced listening to my aura a lot. This came partly through my studies and experience in tantra.

After you decide who you want to be and start practicing being that person, you receive new intelligence in your energetic field. You will know this because you will resonate with your gut feeling. Your decision making will become more and more intuitive. This is the key to your guidance. Being led by the aura surrounding you which is connected to everything else in the universe. The reward is huge when you follow your gut feeling!

HOW CAN I KEEP MYSELF ALIGNED AND CLEAR IN MY AURA?

This is a key tip to keeping your energy in harmony. Live in your aura and don't get sucked into places or people that don't radiate the same vibration. Nature has the ability to harmonise energy between the universe and self. If you feel distracted all the time, like you're doing things that don't serve you, you're better off moving your energy into a natural state first. What I mean is that when we are busy, overwhelmed or running through all our daily tasks, we get lost in everything we do, rather than being balanced.

There is a simple and effective way to reset; get some nature bathing in! Being in nature allows us to ground or root. One way to harmonise yourself is to sit next to a tree and let the tree enter into your aura. The tree is already in harmony with everything in the universe so it will clear your aura from the overwhelming things that are affecting you and bring you more into balance with the universe and yourself. Do this until you feel better and harmonised again. In Spanish culture they have something called 'siestas'. A siesta is basically a nap, normally taken in the afternoon after lunch. There is a quality in napping that magically resets the energetic field.

When you feel overwhelmed or overstimulated, one of the fastest and easiest ways to reset is to have a nap. When you wake up from a nap, there is a moment of choice. You can go back to the same thought patterns you were in before the nap, or you can take a different path. I would like to invite you to take that different path.

Nowadays we are used to living in apartments. There is enough space to live in. But there is not enough space to freely vibe and be with yourself in your own energetic field. This is because we are surrounded all the time by someone else's aura, which may not be totally synced with your own energy. One of the places where we normally spend 8 hours a day is in bed. Just like with the tree, we are sleeping near someone else (think about all the walls in houses and apartment blocks, where we are surrounded by many people without seeing them) and our aura will begin to pick up energy vibrations from those nearby. Ever wondered why you wake up some mornings feeling more drained?

Perhaps you slept right next to someone suffering from depression and you didn't even know it due to the wall in between! It's important to choose a place to sleep that is not surrounded by others you are not in alignment with. Don't tolerate sleeping in close proximity to someone who drains your energy. Our aura stretches out four metres in all directions around us, all the time. This gives you an idea of what and who enters into your energetic field.

GRATITUDE AND ITS CLOUDS

Gratitude is the basic practice to change our paradigms. Being thankful for all we have. Being thankful that what we dreamt of yesterday has now become part of our reality. There is actually an energetic gratitude cloud that already exists. Being thankful creates an energetic gratitude cloud around us. This personal cloud has access to the bigger energetic cloud that already exists. Remember, like attracts like. By connecting to the bigger cloud we become part of the bigger collective which enables us to receive more. When we are in gratitude mode we are also in receiving mode, therefore the key to the universe is simply to ask.

In other words, if you say thanks to your mother for what she is doing, she will feel appreciated and more connected. She will feel ready to give you more of the same feeling. So you can create a field that receives more and more.

The second key is persistence. The invitation is to have your own prayer by being thankful. Create a space where you feel at peace, a space for a meditative state. Write down your gratitude. The reward is huge.

EXPERIMENTS:

- Play nice calming music. Create a meditative sitting space. Breath deeply in and out three times. Write down your gratitude for as long as you like.
- Afterwards, close your eyes and imagine a cloud full of gratitude around your body. Write down how you feel about this experience.
- Write 10 **SMARTF** goals for one year's time.

Forgiveness

Forgiveness is one of the most beautiful and rewarding practices that we can do in our life. To forgive is to give *for* something. To create freedom from emotions that no longer serve us. To allow freedom to enter our energetic field. To change our emotions about ourselves and the collective. To open up and show up for the better. It works on the personal and collective level as well. To let yourself be guided by different electronic motions, different emotions. When I have anger towards somebody or I am feeling angry in a situation I tie myself to emotions that are not constructive. It happens automatically. Basically the angrier I get, the more I get involved energetically with that experience. As a result, I receive more of it. My anger attracts similar experiences into my life. If I can forgive, I can set myself *free* from this experience instead.

There is this beautiful tradition in Hawaiian culture. It is called *Ho'oponopono*. I have never been to Hawaii myself but I was given the following knowledge. When angry family members or friends had been fighting, they had the practice of creating a circle and would sing Ho'oponopono together. Nana Veary outlines her culture's traditions in her book 'Change We Must'. She shares: *'Historians documented a belief that illness was caused by breaking kapu (the spiritual laws) and that the illness could not be cured until the sufferer atoned for this transgression, often with the assistance of a praying or healing priest. Forgiveness was sought from the gods or from the person with whom there was a dispute'.*[5]

I have heard that the translation of Ho'oponopono means: 'I am so sorry, Please forgive me, I love you and I thank you'. This is one beautiful way that I suggest to release the energetic knots. There are many other ways you can approach this.

All emotions are welcome. However, we don't want to get stuck in emotions that radiate or manifest the same situation again and again. Often, the experiences that we have had in the past are not the ones we want to experience in the future. To do that we have to break the chain of these past experiences. In other words, when you are angry, mad, disagree or have any destructive emotion you are radiating that energy in your own energetic field. Imagine that each painful experience we have forms a chain that keeps us stuck in a repeating loop. The invitation is to open these chains one by one as soon as we are aware of them. The first step is to recognise them. You may have heard of the phrase 'when it's hysterical it's historical'. This means that when we experience intense destructive emotions, we know there is a chain that needs to be broken from our past. The invitation in this chapter is to use forgiveness to break these chains.

5. Veary, Nana (1990) Change We Must: My Spiritual Journey. Institute for Zen Studies. p.45

HOW?

The invitation is to write a list of people that you feel energetically triggered by. There are people in our lives that we feel we need to have a conversation with. Often it may not be possible to have that conversation with them, for a variety of reasons. One of those reasons is because we don't feel able to. Some of these people may have created heavier chains and with others it may be slightly smaller energetic chains that we feel. I invite you to write a list of these people.

Now, I invite you to write a letter to each of them. Perhaps it's to your grandparents, or parents. Maybe it's your brother or sister. It could be a lover, an ex co-worker or anybody else.

To begin, first write down why you are thankful for them, and find the reason. There will definitely be a reason to be thankful. Think of the times that you spent together and remember all the good memories. Thank them for co-creating all those moments. When you are done with being thankful, the second part is to write why you feel sorry and where you made mistakes in your relationship with them. It is important to acknowledge what you are sorry for. Finish writing both your thankfulness and what you are truly sorry for. After that, it's time to write and express the feelings you have towards the situation that arose and the resentment that built.

In this part, it's important to begin every resentment with the words *'I forgive you for....'*. Explain with clear language how you feel and why. The more clear, the more powerful it will be. If there are many feelings that you experience, be honest and express them. Take this experiment seriously. The final part of the letter is sharing why and how much you love them. This is a great opportunity to cleanse your energetic field. You are opening your chains that we mentioned before with this experiment so you can feel lighter. Feel into it. Write to everybody on your list. This is such a powerful experiment and it opens up so many aspects of life. It is truly unbelievable what can be released through this practice. After you write the letter(s) you keep them. By writing your letter you have already opened these ties, and broken these energetic chains. Most of the time you will not want to share it with others, and that is often the right thing to do. However, if you want to meet that person and tell them that you forgive them, then create that space. Make an appointment with them in the most neutral space. Not in your house and not in their house. When you meet, first check in with them how they feel and what is happening in their life. Let them talk. Through that you create a safer space for them to receive what you want to share. Tell them about this book that you are reading and share your experiences. Mention this experiment.

Ask if they want to listen to the letter you wrote to them. Before you start reading the letter, ask them if they are willing to listen until the end of the letter. Let yourself be vulnerable. Let yourself be humble. Read the letter. Tell them that you forgive them to open all the energetic chains. Tell them that you are open for future life experiences together (if this is the case). After you read the letter, ask them how they feel. If they want to explain, listen to them and give them space. However, if they start to manipulate you out of your experience, keep your integrity and tell them that you already forgive them. Most of the time, the person is not available or you don't want to do this in person with them. In this case, you create a ceremonial space for yourself and energetically invite them in. Read the letter to them. Forgive them and give yourself permission to be free.

When I did this for the first time the reward was incredible for me. I had a lot of pain with my mother. I told her all the stories that I created from my childhood including why I felt she was guilty. She listened to me. We had dinner in a nice restaurant. I can still remember it like it was yesterday. We reconnected after that and we have a better relationship now even though we live in different countries. This needed to be done. Do it for yourself!

GIVING AWAY

Another experiment to create a space for cleansing includes giving items away. I learned to keep the things that I liked even though I no longer used them. In Chapter 7 I shared the practice of giving away in order to create space to receive more. Here, I invite you to give things away to feel lighter. It is so simple. If you give away clothes that you don't wear, you will release energy that is being occupied by those unused items. As you know, as soon as you do this, the universe will provide new things to fill that space. The more harmonised you are, the more the things that you receive will be in harmony with you. I believe that many of us have shoes and clothes that are really nice. They provide authentic expression and are special. But do we use them as much as they deserve? Maybe you have items that are slightly too small or slightly too big or not really your style anymore. I am sure that there is somebody in your network who would use them more than you. Most importantly, the motivation for this exercise is to clear out old energy.

> *THE JOY OF GIVING AWAY IS*
> *THE JOY OF FREEING YOURSELF*

By giving away you are actually cultivating the mentality of abundance. Since you know that there is enough in the universe, you can let it go. The art of letting go is the art of freedom.

Forgiving and giving away are the same vibration in terms of energy. By releasing, you create a space to receive. If you feel stuck, it could well be time to forgive others. You deserve to fly. Break the chains and let yourself fly higher. Give away items, you will literally feel lighter.

EXPERIMENTS:

- Play nice calming music. Create a meditative sitting space. Breath deeply in and out three times. Write down your gratitude for as long as you like.
- Write 10 **SMARTF** goals for one year's time.
- Collect all the items that you don't use anymore. Give them to people that can use them.
- Write a list of people that you feel angry, sad or have any heavy or tense energy with.
- Write a letter to each one of the people on the list with the following structure.

1. I am thankful for...
2. I am sorry for...
3. I forgive you for...
4. I love you for...

- Write a forgiveness letter to yourself with the same structure as above and read this to yourself.

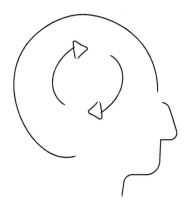

Building Constructive Habits

DECISION MAKING

Making decisions is something that we do constantly. We make decisions all the time: what to eat, what to wear, how to get somewhere and how to work everyday. I used to think a lot about how to make the right decisions. Sometimes the opportunities presented to me were gone before I could even make a decision about it. What I learned later was that making decisions is more important than trying to make the best decision. It's easier to just do it than to think about it for a long time. Making a quick decision is a skill. All successful people are used to making quick and firm decisions. Then, if needed, they change these slowly. The key thing that these people have in common, is that they make things happen after they made the decision! That is such a powerful tool. To make quick decisions you have to follow your gut feeling. Next time that you have to make a decision, feel into it for a few seconds. Listen to your gut. What is it saying? As soon as you know the answer, go for it and have faith. Remember that you will learn from any mistakes.

You will miss 100 percent of the shots that you don't take. If you take a shot, your chance of succeeding is 50/50. After you've made a decision, do your best to accomplish it and create it. We lose a lot of energy in overthinking.

Procrastination is the obstacle that you have to conquer!
To start, I recommend that you make the decision to make more decisions. This is the first conscious decision.

One of the important reasons that we don't make decisions is our fear of judgement. Whatever decision you make, people will talk about it. It is important to stay in touch with the right people who will support you. Don't listen to the naysayers. Another reason that we can't make quick decisions is a conflict between the mind, heart, gut and ego. We can practice to learn what part of our body can make the best decision for us. For me I discovered that my gut feeling is the summary of a whole body decision-making.

This is a practice that you have to build, like a muscle. The more you make quick decisions the easier it becomes. We have every day to practice strengthening these decision-making muscles. This muscle is a habit that we want to build. You will use these muscles for the rest of your life.

HABITS OF TRYING AND DOING

What does it mean to try?
What does it actually mean to do something?
Here is the second part of manifesting the right decisions.
The part that successful people all have in common.

There is a chance that in trying you might actually succeed. In fact, you have about a 50/50 chance more or less. When you start to do something, you are literally doing it. One thing to begin doing is to check your vocabulary to see how often you use the word 'try'.

The word 'try' comes with uncertainty. 'It might happen'. 'I tried my best'. The point is to do it rather than see it as 'trying'. When you try, you might fail. In doing, there is no failure. It's important to understand if you really want to do something or not.

I used to 'try' things when I was not sure. It's ok to try something and find out that you actually don't want to do that thing in the end. You still have space to say no. Still you can try. It's good to know that doing and trying have different meanings. We get too wrapped up in trying, rather than taking the leap and just doing it. Learn to show people what you have done rather than telling them what you are trying to do.

- Make a list of things that you want to do.
- Make a list of things that you want to try.

Feel into these two small experiments and see, what are the differences? Write down your discovery. Bring the habit of doing into your daily life.

PERFORMANCE ATTITUDE

Ask yourself the following questions:

- How do you perform in your life?
- Do you perform with half of your energy?
- With doubt and fear?
- Do you perform out of love and faith?
- Are you performing at full power?
- How often do you go all in?
- How often are you being the best version of yourself?

If I want to achieve a goal I put all my focus and energy into it. All the goals I have achieved I put full effort into. Most of the time, having half of my focus and energy isn't enough to reach the final point. The goal isn't to be the first or the best but to reach the finish line. We have to learn to use 100 percent of our focus and energy to achieve our desired goals. When we use our full energy it already becomes fun. It's challenging and nice to accomplish.

You have to imagine there is no way back and the only way is forward. In the book I've already mentioned, Think and Grow Rich, there was a General who burnt his ship when they landed. There was no way back. This is a process I suggest you get used to. By breaking the bridges that give you comfort, you cannot look back or go back. This means that you are going to have to do what you set out to do.

This is the time to give it 100 percent of your performance. Maybe you have to do some learning. Maybe you have to research. But there is no way to go back. This process actually happens naturally when you have a burning desire to make something happen. No matter how difficult or unreachable it seems, we believe it is going to happen and we have faith in it. When we have a burning desire for something it is going to happen anyway. We may not know immediately how. However, 'how' is not important. You will find it along the way.

BURNING DESIRE

We might have a lot of goals and dreams, but usually there is one that really fires us up. I call that firing up, **burning desire**. This particular dream or goal keeps you up the whole night, it continually plays on your mind and feelings. It wakes you early in the morning and propels you through the day. It gives you the energy to go for life. It creates such an energy that you don't know when and how you got tired. A burning desire is a goal that you have faith and love for. It changes your life. It makes you feel energetic and unstoppable. We can figure out what our burning desire is in the following exercise as we don't always have direct access to it. It's a simple experiment and extremely powerful. It is called a **dream-board**. A dream-board is a collection of images to inspire and motivate us.

Do the following to make your own dream-board: Create a board with images of everything that you want to achieve or be. Cut these images out of magazines (the car, the house, the family, the animals and plants you want around you, the travels you want to go on, absolutely everything that is possible for your brain cells to imagine).

You can find more steps of how to create a dream-board at the bottom of this chapter in the experiments section! Hang it in your bedroom, office or some place where you will see it everyday. This will imprint in your subconsciousness. By seeing this dream-board on your wall on a regular basis, you may notice that one of the images becomes more and more exciting to you. This idea, this dream, this goal, starts a fire inside of you. That fire is your burning desire.

Another tip on the dream-board is how to take action on our imaginary future that we have created on the wall. For example, a car that we have put on the board. The next action would be to go to the dealership that sells this car. Try the car. Get excited while you're in it, and tell yourself 'This is mine!!!' Experience it, feel it, and your burning desire will catch a light! This is a tool to activate that fire inside of you.

The other way to understand what your burning desire is, is to think about what you want to do all the time. Answer the following questions:

- What would you do if nobody would pay you?
- What does your dream life look like?

Burning desire is a state of being that makes you work full power. It's a state of mind that you want to do everything to get there. If you don't know what that is yet, no problem. When it arises in your life nothing will stop you. If you already experience burning desire, you know what I am talking about. Don't let others' opinions and judgements get in your way! Just to remind you, you might have multiple burning desires over time.

RISK

Answer the following questions:
- What is a risk?
- How often do I take risks?
- Is it acceptable in our society to take risks?

I don't know about you, but I grew up in a society that risk taking is seen as a stupid move. People would say, *'Hey, why do you take risks so often?'* I only took risks once or twice a year!

What I actually learnt is that taking risks is a really good move. Risks expand my reality. So let's get to the core of what risk is. We all have a safety zone, which we know how to function in. Living in our comfort zone is the easiest thing to do and the path of least resistance. Normally, this is where you get your income. It's where you feel emotionally safe. It is where you feel the most comfortable to move around in. Outside this comfort zone is unknown. Whatever you want to do outside this zone may seem scary. It comes with insecurity, because you don't know how to take the first step. Some steps may take you far away from your comfort zone and others may be closer.

When you start moving outside of your comfort zone, you start learning about it. It gives you new information. When you take the step and start to explore this new area, it will soon also become part of your comfort zone. It is possible that sometimes we take a HUGE step and it doesn't feel good. That is also okay. This allows you to realise which smaller steps need to be taken first in order to take bigger steps and feel comfortable. Taking risks expands your reality. Jump into risk taking, because there is so much opportunity to discover.

Risk is a good thing, if it feels constructive. Let the excitement guide you. Actually it is good to know that *excitement is the other side of anxiety.*

So if you want to have an exciting and joyful life, you might want to risk more. Starting with small steps allows the muscle of risk taking to grow and get stronger. In my opinion decision making and risk taking go hand in hand. Make more decisions that excite you. Yes, you heard it right. Make more decisions that excite you! Get involved with full energy and learn how to make it happen. Keep asking yourself the important question: *'What would I do if I was not afraid?*
- then act accordingly!

HOW RICH PEOPLE DEAL WITH MONEY

It's good to understand and know how rich people handle money. Here when I say 'rich people' I am talking specifically about high income earners. Napoleon Hill wrote a whole book about how rich people approach money. What's more powerful than reading however, is to work with rich people in order to learn how to deal with money. All the different aspects from learning how to deal with banks or how to build a business or when and where you can borrow and loan. Even with their working methods and processes, you will absorb faster being with them than reading about it. If you spend enough time with rich people you will slowly observe their mentality and their way of dealing with money.

I learned quite a lot from rich people. I learned how to save money. I used to earn a lot of money and I used to spend most of it in a day too.

What I learned was to have a savings account or a safe that I don't always have access to. When I was talking with one of my rich friends, he told me that he saves ten percent of his income every month. First he saves, then he knows how much money he has. In 2-3 years' time, that amount grows exponentially.

The other skill I learned is how to decrease my expenses. I learned that I don't have to earn a lot to live well. But if I avoid unnecessary payments then my savings will grow fast. One of the biggest expenses for everybody is their home. We pay a lot for shelter. Since I changed my approach, I live in bigger spaces, in nicer spaces and pay less. Start to work more closely with rich people and let them influence your behaviour and attitude towards money.

EXPERIMENTS:

- Play nice calming music. Create a meditative sitting space. Breath deep in and out 3 times. Write down your gratitude for as long as you like.
- Write 10 **SMARTF** goals for one year's time.
- Create your own dream-board. Follow the steps below:
  - Find a couple of life, travelling, house and car magazines. Or anything else that resonates with you.
  - Cut out pictures that you find attractive and create a dream-board.
  - Get a big piece of thick paper or cardboard and some paper glue.
  - Glue the images. Be creative and get weird.
  - Hang the dream-board up in your bedroom or somewhere that you see daily.

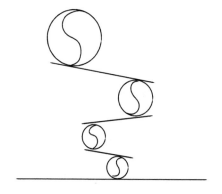

Emotional Balance

In my daily life I meet many people who look for balance and harmony, but what does that actually mean? I also notice that some people try to create balance and harmony in their surroundings. Some strive to create a balance in nature. I guess they feel it is messy, the way it is. Is it just a reflection of their mind?

However when you feel things are out of balance this may be the exact moment that things are falling into place for you and magic is happening. It is actually not that difficult to find balance and harmony and feel into it. It is quite simple, it just takes mindfulness to come to one's life. Just by breathing we can realise what it means to be a part of this magical life. The ocean, the mountains, the birds and all the wonder of that which has manifested. To live and consciously experience the awesomeness that you can recommend to others as well.

Here is a personal story. A few years ago I recall that I didn't want to have kids. This was because I was not satisfied with my life on this planet. How could I bring my beloved to this sorrow? However, this was just my mindset. Today, I do indeed want to have kids to show them the beauty and the magic and the wonder around me. I want to dance with them in the harmonious universe in which we live.

When we get too busy with the inner mental world of analysis and intellectualism, we basically forget why we came here and what we came here to be a part of. Just breathe and observe for a second. Listen to the wind. Listen to the singing birds around you. I have been observing and learning that the universe can bring harmony and balance within itself all the time. We have to remember how to tap into it. Today we see the result of the actions that we did yesterday.

For example, let's look at the pollution in the ocean. What was once 'useful' packaging now results in us eating microplastics inside fish that could cause us disease. We tend to only clean up our waste ourselves when it affects us on a personal level. It's always like that, whatever we do comes back to us. It's like a boomerang. In Buddhism they call it karma. I was introduced to the meaning of the word karma years ago. Karma is the force produced by a person's actions in one life that influences what happens to them in one life or other lives. I found it mind blowing to know that such a law exists. To realise that whatever I do will come back to me whether I want it or not. In one life or another. Once I started to be mindful I observed what was coming back. I started to observe that occasionally karma can be immediate. Sometimes in destructive and sometimes in constructive ways. I started to call tiny constructive ones: karma points. These can be bonuses even. I started to observe that there were random flowers growing in my garden.

Love was coming in. People wanted to invite me for food. Or just to hangout and offer themselves and their beautiful souls. It can be magical. Observing karma helps us know about ourselves and the universe. By understanding this idea of energy and karma I can observe how it balances my life and others' lives.

So what is the first step? If you want to have balance and harmony, do good for yourself and others. It's fascinating what it brings. Just do one good thing that you feel good about for others. Offer somebody a cup of tea, a meal, a good conversation and listen to them. Let them talk to you. When we talk and share our emotions we are balancing energy. Emotions are energetic motions. Energy never gets wasted. It changes its form from one to the other. Emotions are fireworks that can bring you to new levels of play and realisation if you wish.

So let's imagine that somebody is suffering. It's a really good thing because it means that this being wants to have changes. They want to evolve. Suffering is not necessary but it is not necessarily wrong. What will move you from one level to another are the particular emotions. When you experience emotions, listen to them and let them transform you. Sometimes we feel that we have been with certain emotions before. So we experience the same emotion.

That is the best time to observe and receive information from the emotion. Suffering is often labelled as 'bad'. However, it is only emotion telling you something. If you take time and space to receive the information the emotion is telling you, you can move from this place. This means that you are ready for another level. Every single emotion that we experience, is a pearl of wisdom in a being's bag.

FEELING

=

HEALING

Whether you are fat, handsome, rich, poor, short or tall you can experience emotion. The emotion that your being wants to experience, is in a way you choosing it. This is because the emotion that you live is an inner choice. They are not the result of outside life. Nobody can force you to be happy or angry. So actually you are choosing to experience the emotion as you please, when you please.

I have had people telling me that I was blocked before. I want to personally remind you that it is important to be blocked. Me being blocked was clear proof and justification that I was not the person that I wanted to be. The idea is to not erase a side of myself, but to embrace all sides! The invitation is to live in duality and embrace the dark and light side.

If I deny the shadow, it will appear in the material world more and more. The being of who you really are is always with you. As long as you only want to live half of yourself, only the good, only the nice, only the generous, you are not in your whole being. Do you only want to live with one eye and deny the fullness of who you really are?

I notice that most of us want to be only gentle; to be seen as a good person, attractive, helpful. We didn't come here to just do all the time, but to experience being.

"We are not human doings we are human beings"
- Dalai Lama

The moment you experience your full being you are also in touch with the divine. Then you find the meaning behind doing things and you are motivated to do them. You then do things not because of the result, but because doing it is important.

It's actually all fun and games. It's only play, like a baby born who wants to do things because it's free to do. It's fun to experience, to create, to enjoy life. To start enjoying life is to start balancing your emotions. We do not do things for personal gain but instead do them for *the pleasure of playing.*

I know when things get serious it's difficult to come back to this notion. In reality when shit hits the fan we forget about this joyful, pleasurable and playful state, yet what we desire most is to come back to this unity.

'Just give me inner peace' we may say to ourselves, *'I don't need any more stress'.* This is the perfect moment to just breathe and come back to duality. To accept the dark and light inside of us. You will realise that when we experience stress, we can also experience peace at the same time, because we can realise that we have actually created the stress for ourselves. We have actually subconsciously chosen everything! So to understand the duality is to understand the emotions and what they are here for. To pick our pearls of wisdom from every single emotion that we are experiencing. This is being human. Feet on the grass, head in the stars.

MANTRA

In different cultures and religions there is the practice of chanting mantras. For some reason it feels good. Muslims chant everyday with prayer beads as do the Catholics. Hindus have Mala beads. In fact every religion has their own beads, each with unique names. Words have the power of manifestation. Repeating a mantra or a set of words is using the power of incantation to reach your subconscious mind. If you don't believe something and you repeat it a hundred times a day, you will start to believe in it within your subconsciousness. If you start writing it, it will cause you to think about it. This then gets plugged in your subconsciousness. It's powerful work to access that information. If you say 'I am healthy' a hundred times a day or 'I am rich' a hundred times a day, you will start to believe in it. This will also enable you to become more open to receiving those qualities. I personally wrote 'I am rich' for at least five years every day.

Words have their own power of creation. Words and language are one of the strongest forms of expression. We express ourselves to each other and to our own being. With language, we can translate our emotions into words and transfer them to others. If you explain to somebody that you are sad, this passes on to them and they also get the feeling of it. We can transfer the energetic motions from one being to the other using language and we can also translate our emotions to the universe.

As I mentioned above, we choose our emotions too. This is an inner choice that we make subconsciously. Our creations in life start from the emotion that we feel and experience, which is then translated into words of thought. So what I invite you to start doing is to consciously choose the emotions, thoughts and words you send to the universe. As a result, you will begin to receive the emotions, thoughts and words you have consciously chosen.

Mantras are *consciously chosen words*. The more you repeat them, the more they emphasise the feelings and concepts behind them. This has a huge impact. The power of words is in the present moment of using them. They actually activate your subconscious to change your beliefs, even though you might not believe in them in the beginning.

Years ago I started to write 'I am rich'. It started at 50 times a day, then 100 times a day. It changed my conception around abundance and money. Today I feel rich and abundant. The invitation is for you to start writing 'I am rich'. You don't have to believe it, just write it every day for a month and see what happens for yourself.

When you write, you activate your imagination, and thus activate your receiving mode. During covid-19 I asked my beloved to write I am healthy and look at it. She changed her state of health in a week. I have been observing this. It really helps: if you write 'I am rich' or 'I am healthy' and hang it somewhere you can see. It will hack in your deeper subconscious mind.

> *IF YOU WANT TO RECEIVE LOVE,*
> *WRITE 'I AM IN LOVE'.*
> *IT WORKS!*

BALANCE

To create more balance in your life I invite you to observe your behaviour. Feel into it. If you ever hurt somebody, step forward and apologise sincerely. First, let the flame settle down. Then, tell them that you are not perfect and you understand what you have done. Surround yourself with people who tell you that you can make it. If you have a friend or family member who always tells you your ideas will not work, or has negativity towards your choices, get distance from them. Get distance from the ones who want to limit you. Coaches can help to guide you through your limiting relationships if you desire and find balance. It's amazing to have a coach, somebody that you look up to, like a mentor. Your surroundings and environment and the people in your circles of influence are important. Choose them wisely. Remember to observe how you talk to yourself!

Ask yourself the following:
- Do I motivate myself?
- Do I make myself lazy?
- Which part of myself is talking and from which angle?

The most important person that you talk with is yourself! Observe all of the different aspects and perspectives you have of yourself. It's fine to notice that things may contradict themselves, but there should be no fight.

EXPERIMENTS:

- Play nice calming music and write your gratitude for 5-10 minutes.
- Write 10 **SMARTF** goals for one year's time.
- Write 'I am rich' 50 times every day, for one week. Or if you like, why not try writing it every day for a month?
- Write 'I am rich' and hang it somewhere you can see.
- Look at the picture on the next page. What do you see? Ask another friend to look at it. Ask them what they see. See if you see the young lady or the older woman. Which one is the better version or are they just different perspectives?
- Write down 5 things about yourself where you find duality or conflicting views. Are you inclined to opt for one side or can you encompass both? Where do these appear in your life?
- Think of your own personal mantra. For example, 'I am rich', 'I am love', 'I am free', 'I am stable'. Write this every day for at least five minutes.

Victim

I would say that it's common nowadays to be a victim. I believe that we live in this imaginary world. An imaginary world that is divided into two groups of people. Nice people and mean people. Mean people hurt nice people and nice people are the victims. Victims of war, victims of our parents, our schooling, our society, global warming, pollution, governments and so on. You can feel sorry for yourself for just about anything. You can also blame pretty much everyone, often on behalf of others. It's actually an easy method to try to relieve the symptoms of being a victim, to blame something or someone else. It's great to chat as a victim. Victims love chatting and sharing their tragic stories. How they've been hurt and how much they feel sorry for each other. The solidarity of "Yeah, I know" and "I get you". Being a victim creates a bond between people. They feel empathy towards each other, telling each other how shitty life is. They can drink together and have these compelling chats. Some people with a victim mentality may even spin false tales to create more sympathy.

However, even the 'mean' people who hurt others also experience the feeling of being a victim. For example, take a manager at a corporate company, they may have thoughts such as: 'Look at all these lazy people. They just don't work hard enough and I'm left to do all the work'.

Another example may be someone who's wealthy and who creates the idea that everybody wants to take their money from them. If we look closer we can see that there is actually a lot more to discover. I discovered some people create problems to be a part of the 'nice' people group. By doing this, they create more and more enemies in order to belong to the camp of 'nice' people. First, let us look at exactly what it means to be a victim. This begins with the feeling that others are responsible for what is happening to us. There is a feeling of powerlessness and that things are out of our control.

This may include:

- Not feeling responsible for our own life and choices
- Feeling unstable
- Feeling that life is against us
- Feeling attacked when someone offers us feedback
- Blaming others
- No self reflection
- Feeling bad or sorry for ourselves

Being a victim is a choice. Even a choice that may be made unconsciously. We might just blame things and people because that is what our parents did and our grandparents before them. We often don't even know that these subconscious ways have been passed down, of how we should feel and why.

It is easy to create stories that we are a 'nice' or 'good' person, which makes us feel good.

The other side of the equation is to be responsible. To take control and realise our choices. We have to take action in places that we want to change. First we must plant the seed of constructive action, to stop blaming and fighting from now on. It is never too late to stop seeing yourself as useless or helpless, but instead to become a creator, a change-maker. Being responsible means to be stable and process your emotions. I invite you to start living the change that you dream of.

MODES OF BEING A VICTIM

I used to use my victim personality to justify my choices and to feel right about things. I would do this over and over. I have to say if you are willing to do this deep work, it makes you feel very uncomfortable. You have to look into old patterns, own them and change them. It is good to remember that things are changing all the time, both in constructive ways and destructive ways. There is always an opportunity to look inside our personal life events. We just have to remind ourselves to keep our eyes and minds open. We have the choice to work on this mentality or to continue blaming others and feeling miserable.

Writing this chapter reminded me of a story that I heard about a shoe company who sent two sales executives to another country separately to do research and start a branch abroad. The first one called back and said it was impossible to work in the country that they were posted in. People there did not know why they had to wear shoes. The odds were stacked against them and profits would be really low. The executive thought that it was better to choose another location to work. However, the other executive called and was super excited. This one explained that this is the best market ever. Nobody wears shoes! If they could make it, they would have a huge market. This colleague believed that they needed more people and money to get things started before other shoe companies would find out and start investing. This shows the first executive had the 'glass half empty' mindset, which is the same as the victimhood mindset. This executive is blaming the country for the possibility of something not working. "No one wears shoes, so this project won't work", is blaming the outside world. The other executive saw the potential where others couldn't see it. One of the tactics to stop being a victim is to start to see life in a 'glass half full' mentality.

Being a victim offers us many things. It is an opportunity to join the camp of 'nice' people. It allows us to blame others for what is happening and not take any responsibility for it.

We can justify our choices and make them look good. For example, I might say to my 'nice' friends at a bar after work, "I work so hard for 40 hours a week because my rent is so high". Here I am justifying what I do in order to fit in. Another mode of being a victim is rationalising. I rationalise what is happening in my life, and tell a story that makes it acceptable. Others can relate to it and feel sorry for me. This feels good. Now I feel part of the 'nice' group and we can have a nice empathic conversation. In other words we just want to earn respect from others and we constantly try to make a good impression. Sometimes our perception of other people's opinions of us is so important that we fall into this spiral of the victim mentality. Whenever we rationalise or justify our life events it is a good moment to look deeper.

AM I GOOD ENOUGH?

This is a question that victims often struggle with.

The answer is YES. As soon as you take responsibility for yourself and your actions of course you are good enough! Then you are able to create your authentic self and everybody can see this. However, victims may want to take you down to be more like them. There is a chance that you will never get out of this loop, if you continue to see others' opinions as superior to your own.

Some people will get cheered up by your dramas, and others will act differently and support you to be more responsible. It's actually a good opportunity to find people who sync up with this new perspective of taking responsibility and rising above others' opinions.

Besides that we have been programmed by the media to understand that we suffer because of 'bad' people. All the time we are reminded of all the 'bad' news and 'bad' events and the people that are contributing to that. Even a lot of top-seller musicians write lyrics about 'bad' people in relationships who cheated us or didn't give us enough love. It is quite the realisation to observe how much we have been programmed to feel the victim mentality. What if you have a choice once and for all to do things differently?!

Ask yourself:
- What does it look like to take control?
- What does it look like to be stable?
- What would it feel like to be the primary creative force in your own life?
- What does it feel like to own your responsibilities and be in your power?

Look at these questions in relation to all the events that are happening in your life. From now on, start to see your part in every single action and take responsibility for it.

How does it feel to be the captain of your own ship? Now is the time to tell everybody in every single situation how exactly you are taking responsibility, and what that responsibility is. You can begin to tell people you are willing to make changes. There are some things you don't need to get involved in, since they are out of your control, and you can't be responsible for them. Now is the time to plant seeds for bigger changes. Will you take this opportunity?

To be responsible is a decision, a decision that will change a lot of results. This decision marks the quality of a true leader. One who creates change for themselves and for the collective.

Being responsible equals no longer blaming others, no longer justifying and rationalising uncomfortable situations and giving them a nice shape. Being responsible is a catalyst for change. The only person who knows what is good and what is not good for you, is you! Take the chance and go for it. The invitation is to feel into what you just read and be aware of your destructive thoughts and feelings. Overcome them with the single decision to become responsible. Make this decision out of love and respect for yourself.

EXPERIMENTS:

- Play nice calming music. Create a meditative sitting space. Breath deep in and out 3 times. Write down your gratitude for as long as you like.

- Write 10 **SMARTF** goals for one year's time.

- Think about the last situation when you tried to justify yourself. Write down your experience, why you did it and how you felt afterwards. What would you have done differently if you took more responsibility?

- Think about the last time you rationalised to yourself. Write down your experience, why you did it and how you felt afterwards. What would you have done differently if you took more responsibility?

- Now that you are deciding to be this new responsible person, what will you do differently in your life? Write this down. How are you going to talk to others about it? Where and with what people will you invest your time?

Think Win-Win

In daily life we make agreements all the time. We make deals all the time, with our family, our loved ones, our colleagues, our boss, and everybody else. But have you ever looked at how and why we do that?

Let's ask ourselves:
- Am I always thinking about winning a good deal?
- Do I want to lose sometimes and give somebody else the win, and the glory and the joy of winning?
- Do I care at all about others when I am making deals?
- Do I think that I can win, while the other person can also win?
- Do I get angry sometimes and make everybody lose? And do I find joy in doing that?

Start answering those questions above and begin to think about it. Basically in life we make one of these agreements below.

WIN/LOSE

LOSE/WIN

WIN/WIN

LOSE/LOSE

Having an understanding of this helps to guide ourselves to a higher energetic field and begins to connect us with the energetic abundance in our life.

WIN/LOSE

Win/Lose is the most common agreement that we deal with all the time. It is the status-quo in the business world. It has been deeply scripted in our society. It comes from the space of neediness and competition. Here is an example of this. There is an apple, either I have it or you have it. It's a mentality that supports poverty. It's where resources are limited. Perhaps we learn this in school and from TV. Many kinds of competitions have only one prize. This actually invites us to be more cruel, more competitive and to learn to fight over things. I still see many spiritual or conscious people who are busy dealing with the same paradigm. So the idea is: if you lose, I will win. This can be totally ok, if we both agree on it.

This paradigm invites us to live in a limited universe and fight for resources. It is climbing the ladder of success by pushing others down. It feels like you are winning, but actually what you are doing is losing the people that you beat. They might even admire you for doing this, but deep in their heart everybody knows the truth, that this is not OK. These people are watching and waiting for you to fail. There is a hidden agenda to watch a successful person lose.

I don't know if this happens for you or not. I remember that I never liked to lose. I would fight hard to win and if I lost, I would get really angry. Let's go further, in its best performance this Win/Lose creates hard competition.

Let me ask you few questions:

- When you marry, who is going to win?
- When you start a new job, who is the winner?
- Starting a new company, who is the winner?

A Win/Lose strategy is a dysfunctional attitude. Today a lot of companies are trying to change it. To create more synergy in order to achieve more. At the very end a Win/Lose attitude will turn into a Lose/Lose one. Because the winner will start losing as soon as others are not willing to support them anymore. The winner will find themselves a loser and try to play differently. From this vantage point, many of them start playing the Lose/Win game to gain some love and respect. If the agreement is to just benefit one side, it's a Win/Lose situation. In the long run it creates distrust and resentment. It will eventually become a Lose/Lose situation.

LOSE/WIN

This one brings to mind what is expected from mothers. They try to give their best to their kids. They sacrifice themselves in order for their kids to grow in a perfect environment. What happens if the kids are always the winner?

They become programmed to win, in the Lose/Win dynamic. However, when entering the real world this is not what they get all the time. These kids are entitled to win. So they are in search of finding people who want to give them that win, like their mothers. Yet, they still want to hang out with winners of course.

So, what about their mothers? Of course they love their mothers but they don't like to hang out with them, because often she is seen as a loser, often because she has put the children first. The children don't want to hang out with losers, they want to hang out with winners and win more and more.

This is actually such a toxic dynamic and relationship. There is also the same dynamic with sugar daddies. They become the stereotype of someone who spends all his money on the beauty of a woman, but there is no dignity and integrity there. Just like mothers that were not appreciated, sugar daddies are not appreciated by their partners. Their partners want to hang out with winners somewhere else. A loser is never appreciated unless by another loser.

However, society is not willing to play the same game all the time and so the kids have to fight. The kids that grew up with the Lose/Win mentality will never overcome those who grew up with the Win/Lose mentality.

This entitlement to win then breeds winners at home but losers outside the home, in society. So they will come back to continue a toxic relationship to win against their parents back in the house. However this is a Lose/Lose paradigm at the end too.

LOSE/LOSE

Think of a divorce. Think of a war between two stubborn headstrong sides that have to deal with each other. They might lose just so that the other won't win. Imagine that you have to share half of your assets. You might think something like this: 'If I'm going to be screwed over, then I will screw you over too'. If nobody wins, you don't mind losing too. This may lead you, for example, when going through the divorce that you would rather sell everything for cheap than give the contents back to the other party. Lose/Lose mentality is a mentality of war. It's the most destructive and often ends in total ruin.

WIN/WIN

Win-Win mentality invites equality and mutual understanding. It's the invitation for peaceful agreement in a safer space where everybody is a winner. I don't need to win if you are losing, better to be supportive and make sure no one is falling off the ladder. With a Win/Win agreement we can build a constructive relationship and in the end, a vibrant society.

A great example of a Win/Win is the sharing of information. If I know how to build and create an amazing life I can share that information with you. Then you can build an amazing life too. In this situation you win how to build and experience your authentic amazing lifestyle. So you win. But I also win when for example we meet. I can taste your abundance and the beauty of your being. When more people have an amazing life we get to experience this together. This ultimately creates safer and safer spaces and places for me, my family and community to grow and enjoy life. That's already a Win/Win. Then you might inspire others to do the same and I might meet and become friends with a person who's inspired by you. Since they have a unique life and viewpoint, I will be privileged to enjoy that life with more wonderful Win/Win people. This mentality of Win/Win just keeps growing, bigger and bigger. Win/Win attitude always multiplies.

Here is another instance. You know how to cook a special pie. You share how to cook that pie with me. I can bake the same pie and you didn't lose anything. We will eat the same pie together and it tastes pretty good.

Win/Win attitude comes from an abundance mentality that there is enough and I don't have to compete. It's a great game to play because it's nice to play, we are raising ourselves up together.

Win/Win sees the world as cooperative and not competitive. Win/Win at its core seeks mutual benefit in human interactions.

HOW TO INVITE A WIN/WIN MENTALITY INTO OUR DAILY LIFE?

If you are not used to this, it can be challenging to start.

It comes with a deep understanding of the other person's needs. Ask the other person in the dynamic these questions.

Listen carefully to their responses to these questions:

- What do you want to achieve with this agreement?
- What are you looking for?
- Can we form an agreement that benefits us both?

This experiment requires us (the person asking the questions) to stay tuned into our true feelings. Often we want to make an agreement and we forget about our true feelings. The next step is to suggest and express your ideas and feelings. Express these in accordance with the others' wants and desires that benefit them, as well as considering your own values and benefits. The other consideration is if there is no deal. That is a deal as well. Sometimes it's just not possible to meet people's benefits while you're meeting yours at the same time. At this point you must learn to step back and say 'Sorry, but I don't have anything to offer you at this moment'.

That shows your integrity and maturity in making deals.

Win/Win is a belief in the third option. It's not about my way or yours. There is always another option or method that we didn't think of. Moreover, it needs time and space to find this third option. I have to admit that in the long run if it's not a Win/Win, it will become a Lose/Lose which we don't want.

EXPERIMENTS:

- Play nice calming music. Create a meditative sitting space. Breath deep in and out 3 times. Write down your gratitude for as long as you like.
- Write 10 **SMARTF** goals for one year's time.
- Think about your life and see what kind of agreements you have with your family, with your partner, with friends, or at your job.
- Think and understand how you can change those agreements to make them beneficial for both of you.
- Make the first Win/Win agreements today.
- Step one: find out what your partner in business/life needs in this agreement through questions.
- Second step: express your needs and feelings.
- Third step: find a way that can meet both people's needs and if not, make no deal.
- Fourth step: double check if you understood correctly what the other person's benefits are. Check you are meeting their benefits in the agreement while also meeting yours.

Vision

Today I am sitting in a café somewhere in Lagos, living my abundant life. I enjoy the sun in the winter and I am sharing this chapter with you, so that you too can live the life you dream. This was my dream life 10 years ago while I was doing a corporate job. Now I am at a milestone in creating the life that I dreamed of. How we vision our future is key in bringing us to the present moment of realising and living these visions.

THE END SITUATION

The end situation means to know where you are going. To visualise the end point and see the path and the way back to where you are now. To be able to feel and break down the steps to the goals you set. I grew up in a mindset knowing where I was. I began saving money to get things done, without knowing exactly where I was going. I didn't know why I was saving or why I was doing things. Once I began first visualising my end points, I could then visualise my way forward. This meant I began to understand why I was doing what I was doing, like saving money.

Imagine that you work hard and do everything to grow and achieve everything you want. You play by the rules and write your goals. After a long journey you realise, *'Oh my!! This is not what I wanted'.*

Or perhaps you think, '*I worked so hard for this so it is definitely better than nothing*'. Or, '*Getting somewhere is better than getting nowhere*'. If you had been able to visualise the outcome in the beginning, perhaps you would have chosen differently.

To explain what I mean above, this sentence from Stephen R. Covey covers it well, '*If the ladder is not leaning against the right wall, every step we take just gets us to the wrong place faster*'. So imagine that you want to go from Sweden to Portugal. You don't use a map and you just follow the south road. You might end up somewhere on the coast either in Italy, Croatia, Greece or Portugal. But if you know exactly where you are going, you can plan your journey correctly. Your vision needs to be specific. I want to ask you to read this part of the book in a place where you can give it your undivided attention. I would like to invite you to find a place where nobody can interact or distract you. If it's warm enough, ideally somewhere in nature. I want to invite you to carry incense with you, a pen and paper or your journal. If you are not in nature play some calming, meditation music for yourself.

When you are in the place where you will do this experiment, read the following instructions:

- Light the incense.
- Play the music or listen to the natural sounds around you.
- *Take a deep breath* and feel the fresh air in your lungs, let it cherish you.
- When you feel calm after a few deep breaths, I invite you to close your eyes. Read the following paragraph in this same calm, meditative state. Read the words 10 times slower than you would normally read, pausing between sentences and noticing the sensations in your body. Visualise yourself sitting in your dream car. Driving in the streets of a city. There is a parking spot that you want to park in. After you park the car, you see yourself in the mirror and you realise that you are in your seventies. I want to invite you to look around and see the trees and the other cars and people as they are passing by. *Take a deep breath* and feel what you feel. You're parked in front of a cinema and you are going to watch a movie and you observe many people excited outside. When you look at the board you realise the movie is about your life. There are friends and family in front of the door. I want you to imagine that you walk towards them and they greet you and show enthusiasm to watch the movie with you.

They are waiting for you. Imagine that you walk towards them. *Take a deep breath.* They greet you and are very happy to accompany you to watch this movie together. Take some time to greet them and meet them. There is a warm feeling, being there together. Walk through the halls and stairs of the cinema. Then find yourself walking inside the cinema room and finding your seat. *Take another deep breath.* The movie starts and shows a baby born on its birthday. You are now watching yourself being born and coming to this planet. Your family is there. Watching yourself growing up. One year old, two years old and so on. *Take another deep breath.*

- Experience yourself watching the first 10 years of your life. Going to school perhaps. Then as a teenager. Perhaps you do some sports. Maybe meeting your first love. All the success that you experienced and all the failures. You feel it. Perhaps you will go to college or university or maybe a different path. *Breathe deeply.*

- Now you are entering your twenties. Watching yourself on the screen going through life, watching your relationships, your family, your career or business, let it flow. *Take a deep breath.*

- Let your life story flow. Perhaps you see yourself in your fantasy job and the company that you wanted to start. Your coworkers, siblings and family. There are interviews happening with them in the movie, they are talking about you. What do they say? *Breathe deep.*

- How do they remember you? Now you are slowly getting older and the movie comes towards the end. When the movie finishes and lights turn on, you walk out from the cinema room with your friends. *Take another deep breath.* You want to walk towards your car. Giving last hugs and kisses and moving towards the vehicle. When you enter the car *take another deep breath in.* When you sit in the car, I would like to invite you to close your eyes in your visualisation. *Take another deep breath.*

- Gently open your eyes and come back to reality. *Take another deep breath.* Stay silent. Write down what you saw about yourself. Write about everything that you appreciate about yourself. Take the time now to write about your vision before going further. This writing is actually a very good starting point to know who you really want to become. You can always check if you are on the right path by knowing the final destination. You can do this often and fill in the gaps on your way. Let your higher consciousness guide you through life and its purpose. We feel most purposeful and powerful when we do exactly what feels correct in our core. This can be your guidance in any choices that you make.

HOW CAN I BREAK DOWN MY GOALS USING
THE END SITUATION?

So the idea is to know where we want to go, but first we must break it down in our everyday life. We need to make it more realistic and check if that works somehow. It doesn't need to make 100 percent sense all the time, but you can make things happen by breaking it down into smaller steps. Your subconscious believes and accepts that you can make it. By breaking it down you actually have a better understanding of what is possible. I always suggest dreaming big. If you aim for a star then you may get to the moon. I want to introduce you to some simple and useful examples.

Imagine that you decide to have £150,000 savings in 5 years' time, we must begin with the following questions:

- How big are your savings now?
- How much can you save per month now?
- Can we start from the end and work backwards to break it down?

Here is how the example works: if you want to have £150,000 in 5 years this means that you would have £100,000 in 4 years, 75,000 in 3 years and so on. This means that you need to save £50,000 in 2 years, which means that you would have £35,000 in 1 year. So you must already have £20,000 in savings now!

I call these taking financial baby steps. On top of this thinking you have to learn how to work with your money practically so that it works for you. To invest your money in places that give you 10-20 percent profit yearly and have multiple sources of income. We will talk about that with more details later. But I hope that the above example clearly shows you how to break down your financial goals in that way.

Ok, so if I don't have £20,000 to start what shall I do? Is it to make your goal a bit smaller and be realistic how much you can save per year? To me it is realistic to save 20 percent of your income.

With this technique you can break down your goals in a 5 year time span and start working on them. It actually works to make baby steps to see what you can achieve back to front.

BABY STEPS

Following the example above. In order to get to £35,000 from £20,000, you need to save £15,000 in 12 months. The question is, what is your income at this moment? Can you save £1000 per month? Can you invest your £20,000 in the way that creates £500 per month extra? The idea is to have £35,000 savings in one year. Below I explain how you break it down in baby steps.

If you are at 20,000 in Month 0, your path could look like this:

Month 12: 35,000	Month 8: 28,800	Month 4: 24,400
Month 11: 33,000	Month 7: 27,700	Month 3: 23,300
Month 10: 31,500	Month 6: 26,600	Month 2: 22,100
Month 9: 30,000	Month 5: 25,500	Month 1: 21,000

The idea is to break it down to baby steps and start being realistic and pushing your limits. Maybe it feels too much but just commit and push yourself to create what feels right to you. If you work for what you dream, the whole universe will open its doors and make things happen.

HOW OFTEN DO I DO THIS?

As long as you are a bit confused about life and your values, it will be difficult to achieve. This above method is a powerful process that will bring you back to the path and understand if you are aligned or not. The technique to break your goals down will help you in every situation. If it is building a house, working in the garden, saving money, building a relationship with someone, by having your baby steps laid out you begin to see and feel that you are getting there. It is really powerful to know where you are at, where you are going and to have milestones, these baby steps are the best milestones.

These baby step milestones can awaken your burning desire. It might be the ultimate force to push you forward in life. It might make you an unstoppable force. If so, just flow. Let the energy from this guide you. Like a surfer dancing on the waves. If you fail sometimes, remember the moment that you were on top of the wave surfing and allow that to ignite the power within you again.

THE WAY YOU LIVE YOUR LIFE NOW IS THE WAY YOU LIVE YOUR LIFE

EXPERIMENTS:
- Play nice calming music. Create a meditative sitting space. Breath deep in and out 3 times. Write your gratitude for as long as you like.
- Write 10 **SMARTF** goals for five years' time.
- Break down your 5 year-time goals in 5 stages of 1 year.
- Make baby steps for every single 5 year goal by breaking it into monthly objectives and see if they need to change so that you can make it happen.

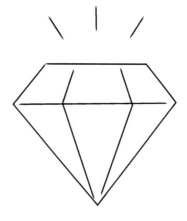

Values

What is at the core of every single decision you have made? What were you attracted to in your decision making process? What do you usually go for?

Our values are normally hidden aspects of our personality that we are not in touch with directly. These affect our relationships, friends, style, food and all the actions that we take. Values are at the core of every single human being. Imagine yourself as an onion with layers. In the core of the onion are the core values. These form the base of our belief systems, which are in the second layer of the onion. So whatever we believe is based on our values. And through that we often unconsciously choose what to believe and what not. The third layer is expectations. Based on our belief systems we expect the world to move in that direction. Whatever aligns with our belief system makes us happy and vice-versa. The fourth layer of the metaphorical onion is our attitude towards life. So our values define our belief system. Our belief system creates expectations for us in the world around us. Our expectations and belief system create our outwards attitude. Finally, our actions come from our attitude. Our actions form the outermost layer of the onion.

Let us look at this as an example. If in my core I think that the earth needs to stay clean and healthy for animals and humans, I might believe that I need to treat the world with respect. I might expect people to have respect for the environment and use resources with a sustainable attitude. As a result I might become a person who loves animals and ecology. I might eat mostly vegan food or I might use biological-sustainable products that don't harm the planet because of this. I may be more conscious of my fossil fuel use and so on.

Another example is if I have love as one of my core values. I might believe that love can help everybody and cure all problems. I expect that people around me will love each other and act accordingly. My attitude is always approaching things with love and positive energy and as a result I act as a loving person who wants to take care of others.

So you might ask, do I have good values?

Notions of 'good' and 'bad' come from a binary way of thinking. What you may think isn't ideal can be the most perfect action at that time. What you may have thought of as good, later you find out wasn't actually that good after all. Therefore, if we can go beyond the binary thinking of good/bad we can begin to align with our values instead. These ideas of 'good' and 'bad' are so embedded in our culture that I invite you to let this idea live in your body for a while.

Core values are qualities such as love, happiness, peace, revenge, sadness, sustainability etc. See the Experiments section below for a longer list of values to choose from.

WRITE AND DETERMINE FIVE OF YOUR CORE VALUES.

1...

2...

3...

4...

5...

HOW CAN I DETERMINE MY VALUES AND CHECK THEM WITH MY GOALS?

It is important to check if we are pointed in the right direction before we start the journey. One of the ways to understand if our goals suit our lifestyle is to check in with our values. If you value community life, your dream shouldn't be to live on a mountain alone.

Or if sustainability is a core value for you, your dream life can't be travelling by airplanes every week around the world. Check your five-year goals alongside your values and see if they are aligned.

HOW DO YOU VALUE YOURSELF?

Here is another concept of how we value ourselves in relation to income. Ask yourself the following questions:

- Does your salary meet your dream lifestyle?
- Do you get enough money for the services that you provide?
- How can you change the way you have income?

I learned through the years that the way that I value myself with money is the way that others value me as well. When I started looking at it, I found out that I valued myself less than I thought, and so did those around me. I experienced working really hard for little money. I experienced my co-workers bullying me and cheating me, because I undervalued myself.

It is a revolutionary moment when you start to value yourself and be radically fair. It is good to ask yourself what would you pay to the person who works like you? It is extremely important to understand the value of the work you do. Do not work for less than is appropriate because opportunities come when you value yourself fairly!

With this change of belief you might find that there are people who want to hire you and they don't have enough money to pay for your services. There are different ways to deal with this. It's good that you know why and how you want to work. Make that clear.

You can work with different payments and can suggest this, for example getting shares or having percentages. You can use the gift economy and get paid for half with something else on top, or they could pay it forward for example. What you must do here is to make sure that they understand what is happening.

PAY IT FORWARD

I have learned that I can do something good for somebody and ask that person to help another person when they get a chance, or another three even! Let's say I work for you for x hours and you can't pay me in full. As part of my payment, I would like to ask you to pay it forward to another three people when you have the opportunity. Tell them to do the same and as the butterfly effect shows, it may well come back to you.

OLD PARADIGM

Years ago I used to work long hours for money. I learned that you work eight hours a day for x amount of money. So forty hours per week, day in and day out, I toiled. I would wake up early in the morning with an alarm. The alarm would snooze until I finally left the bed and jumped in the shower. I had my coffee in the car, running to get in on time for work. I was like a zombie, getting my breakfast at work and only at the lunch break would I get some fresh air.

Then I would eat some food that was not at all fresh or nutritious since I had no time to cook something myself and bring it with me. Mostly I ordered fast food. I worked my way through the day continually looking at the clock till it got to five pm and I could finally go back home.

Most of the time I worked for companies that deep inside, I was not satisfied with. Getting back home I would make myself busy until I slept and didn't spend much money. This was all because I wanted to save. I had a fairly expensive house just to be close to my office but was still rushing all the time. At the end of the month I would receive my work payment and would feel rich for a few hours. I would then pay my rent, expenses, insurance and mortgage for my car. I realised that there was not much left remaining of the money I had earnt. But no worries, of course there was still a little left to buy that fancy pair of shoes that I could show off at my workplace. I would work 15 hours extra next month and every month the same thing happened.

This is my old paradigm. I believed that hours equals money. I thought to myself: 'I can work 12 hours a day so I can earn more'. I would think: 'Oh I'd like a nice pizza tonight, I'll have to work another hour extra tomorrow'. In reality however, I couldn't work more than a certain amount of hours per month. What would keep me going? Yes, that one week holiday in the summer and one week in the winter.

I also noticed that when I felt a bit richer, my only concern was to get a better car. Go to better restaurants. Somehow I wanted to show off. I learned that my skills plus hours make more money. Life was fairly good. But there came a time when I noticed that it was not the way to a good future for me.

Time leverage is limited and I had to think of different leverages. The other leverage that I knew was how to get others to work for me. I paid them for 8 hours of work and if they could earn £20 per hour, inclusive of the costs that they make, I would actually pay them £15. I would earn £5 profit from their work. If I could create a company where 100 people worked for me I would be seeing 800 hours' work per day happening. This I could never do on my own. This method can be fair and moral or entrap employees into modern slavery terms.

The other leverage is if I created a music album for example. I might work hundreds of hours. My music album might be a killer like some good artists and then I would get income from every sale, a steady passive income over time. Think of Michael Jackson albums in the best case. The same goes for writing a book.

One other leverage is network marketing. Since everybody gets a percentage from each other's effort. These are just different ways of looking at how I could get money using different leverages. Some people use money as leverage to create more money. Think of investments. To use money as leverage and get an annual increase per year. However each of them can be constructive or destructive. All these leverages are different ways of how to create passive or active income. The way that I see the world, each of us needs to have multiple sources of income based on our character and values.

EXPERIMENTS:

- Play nice calming music. Create a meditative sitting space. Breath deep in and out 3 times. Write your gratitude for as long as you like.
- Write 10 **SMARTF** goals for five years' time.
- From the list below choose and determine five of your core values. Check your goals alongside your values to see if they are aligned.

VALUES

Abundance   Acceptance   Adventure   Belonging   Charity Communication Community Compassion Competition Courage Equality Ethics Faith Financial Wealth Forgiveness Freedom Gentleness Grace Happiness Health Honour Honesty Humility Humour Joy Justice Knowledge Love Leadership Loyalty Originality Passion Peace Perfection Power Religion Resilience Revenge Risk Sadness Safety Sensuality Stability Self-Discipline Status Support Sustainability Taking charge Tradition Truthfulness Vulnerability Wisdom Youthfulness etc.

- Write down a leverage in your life that you use at this moment to earn money. Write down how this is constructive or destructive for you / or others?
- Write down a leverage that you would like to use more, how would you do that?

Sex Magic & Manifestation Masturbation

I read many books and followed several courses about success. However, there is not much that is dedicated to the link between sexuality and manifestation. Sometimes I read that having the right partner increases your chance of success. I want to bring awareness that sexual energy is a superpower in this regard. We can create new life through our orgasm. On a physical level it is quite intense what our body goes through. Of course, we find it enjoyable, otherwise why would we do it? To gather all your life force energy and let it flow with another being is a special activity in life. There is nothing so profound as being in an orgasmic state. No matter what and where and how, the majority of us are able to participate in this profound act of creativity. Accessing sexual energy is a portal to manifestation. We all are able to create and manifest new life. New life as a baby born or a new life for ourselves.

If we overcome our fears, it's easy to create and blossom. What I want to share with you is that in the moment of orgasm the whole universe is on your command to create. Since we are the creators and creatures at the same time. We can use our own power as a creator. To realise this superpower of creation, you have to make yourself ready for it.

As we have discussed, everything is an energy. So let me break this to you, sex energy is one of the powerful forces we possess as physical manifestations of source energy. Think about it, sexual energy literally creates life.

SEXUAL TABOOS

Energy cannot be good or evil. Energy is energy. However, it can be utilised with good or bad intentions and it can also be wasted away. We hear in different cultures that sex is evil. We are told that we should not talk about it or engage in it, but that is just social conditioning. Sexual energy is some of the most powerful energy inside us that we can harness. So let's look directly at this. Do you know that constant daily masturbation or meaningless hook-up sex involves building up your sexual energies and letting them waste away? There is nothing wrong with that. However, those that wish to manifest their desired life powerfully can consciously retain and entertain their sexual energies. Remember the basic Law of Attraction formula:

$$DESIRE + INTENTION + STRONG\ EMOTION = MANIFESTATION$$

Basically, sexual energy is a direct manifestation of this formula, it's considered to be the highest excitement you can experience in a human body.

HOW CAN I USE MY SEXUAL ENERGY TO MANIFEST?

When I was studying tantra and magic I learned about sex magic in combination with manifestation. I have come across many methods of manifestation masturbation and sex magic. I will share two methods which can be harnessed, solo, as a couple, or with multiple partners. It's also ok if your partner doesn't want to participate. However it's more powerful if you both take part in it. Before we step into this practice I want to mention that I am aware of people's conditioning around masturbation. Basically, conscious masturbation is an act of love. Manifestation masturbation is creating life force with your hands. As soon as you start doing this, the whole universe will respond and your life will change.

MANIFESTATION MASTURBATION

Manifestation Masturbation is a practice that can easily be done. There are also other ways to manifest that I will share with you in this book. Let's look at the following steps below in how to achieve this powerful practice.

- Set an intention. It is important to have a clear smartf intention or goal that you decide so you can prepare this space for creation and manifestation masturbation. It is more effective to have one intention than many. You can use a piece of card, postcard or make something creative for this purpose. Write it down as a **SMARTF** goal.

- Create a ceremonial space. Light a candle, play calming music. Feel yourself in the space and stay open. Make the room temperature comfortable, so you can get naked in it. Have some water, fruit and chocolate to snack on.

- Close your eyes for a moment and imagine yourself in a way that you have achieved the goal already.

- Now is a good moment to activate your kundalini energy. You can simply start with moving your body and breathing from the root chakra and move one by one to the crown chakra (see the index for more references). Use breath, sound and movement.

- Use some oil to play with your body. Massage yourself. Explore all of your body including your genitals. Be creative and keep your heart open. Breathe, make sound, and move your body. Do everything slowly.

- Start to masturbate. Stay present. Breathe. Fantasise about your intention if you want to fantasise. Stay in connection with your body and the sensations. Keep the ecstatic current running.

- Use three pillars of enjoyment: make a sound, move your body and breathe.

- When you feel that you are close to an orgasm, read your smartf goal and affirm your intention by focusing on the third eye (see glossary for more information). Hold a single focus on your visualisation.

- Imagine that you are living that dream intention and keep moving the energy.

- If you can circulate your energy, circulate it. If you want to orgasm, feel free to do it.
- It is important to listen to the messages that we receive from our divine. So if you hear that you have to make a phone call or send an email or do other practical things, do it after your practice.
- <u>Have fun!</u>

SEX MAGIC

Sex magic is a duo+ practice for those who want to manifest with a partner/s. It is a spiritual practice of many in history. This spiritual practice uses sexual energy to manifest matter in the physical world if you so desire.

Follow the steps below:
- Set an intention with your partner. It is important to have a clear smartf intention or goal that you decide together so you can prepare this space for creation and sex magic. It is more effective to have one intention than many. You can use a piece of card, postcard or make something creative for this purpose.
- If your partner/s don't want to participate, it is possible to set an intention on your own, which you hold in mind while present with them. However, it is important to tell them that you're setting this intention.
- Commit to staying present during the ritual. Presence and intention invite sacredness into the space of ritual.

- Create a ceremonial space. Light a candle, play calming music. Feel yourself in the space and stay open together. Make the room temperature comfortable, so you can get naked in it. Have water, fruit and chocolate to snack on.

- Sit in meditation for a few minutes together and breathe deep down into the belly. Now is a good time to name your intentions out loud, to vocalise your boundaries, fears and desires. After each conversation simply reflect them back to each other or say thank you, Aho!

- Close your eyes for a moment and imagine yourself in a way that you have achieved the goal already.

- Start to eye gaze for a few minutes and breathe together to get more connected. It's a good moment to activate your kundalini energy. You can simply start with moving your body and breathing from the root chakra and move one by one to the crown chakra. Use breath, sound and movement.

- Use some oil to play with each other's body. Massage each other. Touch each other's body including genitals. Be creative and keep your hearts open. Breathe, move and make sounds. Do everything slowly. Let the erotic energy move you within spoken boundaries.

- If you feel like merging, this is the time. Stay present.

- Use three pillars of enjoyment; breathe, move your body and make sound. Do it as slowly as possible. The slower the better. Affirm your intention by focusing on the third eye, holding a single focus on your visualisation.

- When you feel that you are close to orgasm, read (if you've placed your **SMARTF** goal someone where you can see), speak or whisper your smartf goal out loud and imagine that you are living that dream intention and keep having sex. Keep affirming your intention within your third eye. Hold the visualisation. You can slow down even more by concentrating on the flow and detail of each little movement. Make it subtle. The more excitement and feeling you have, the stronger the manifestation is.

- If you can circulate your energy, circulate it. If you want to orgasm, have an orgasm.

- Enjoy it and have fun.

- It is important to listen to the messages that we receive from our divine. So if you hear how you should take action, make a phone call, send an email or do other practical things, then you must do this afterwards or as soon as possible.

EXPERIMENTS

- Play nice calming music. Create a meditative sitting space. Breath deep in and out 3 times. Write your gratitude for as long as you like.

- Write 10 SMARTF goals for 5 years' time.

- Plan your first manifestation masturbation and then do it.

- Plan your first sex magic ritual and then do it.

Manifestation Meditation

As I mentioned before, we have electromagnetic fields around each of us. In some cultures they call it an aura. It is the structure of every single being. It is a field full of energy. This is an energy field of luminous radiation surrounding a person as a halo, which is imperceptible to most human beings. This aura is full of motion. We as humans experience those motions and we call them emotions. Energetic motions. This structure is also filled with information. Information about you and people around you. This information is about events that you have experienced and people that you are in touch with. It's about the landscape that you live in. It's about the people that you visit. It's about people that you meet daily, and the ones that you only met once.

The information contained in this aura dictates new experiences as well. If, for example, you randomly meet someone new and you think 'Oh this person seems just like someone else I met recently', this is not a coincidence! This energetic field defines what you are open for and what you are not open for. In this way the universe will fill this energetic field with what's already in it. Which makes it super simple to work with. Not working on this aura is basically getting the same that you have now. So if you are happy with what you have now, it's ok to just live your life but as a creator you can also start changing it.

It's a profound moment, the second that you realise that you can change the information in your electromagnetic field. You can change the emotions and you can start to work on them. You begin to realise and understand and accept who you truly are. You are not actually changing who you are, you are accepting your true nature!

When I learn to accept who I am, I can start to create from that point onwards. This is an act of self love and growth. If I deny who I am, I can't change what I receive. So I am going to learn to love who I am and start to live in the presence of myself and enjoy being that person.

It's important to find the best version of myself, and not to try and be somebody else! To feel into every single action that I take and feel if that's the right thing to do or not. To tune in with my gut and tune into my I. When I begin to feel content with being who I am, I start to be the captain of my own ship.

I promise that every single one of us has the power to create. I experience this strongly when I meet people who create their own life. They embody the motto of *'your faith is your future'!*

A concept that we have of ourselves might be a lie. We might create this lie in order to not get hurt and to make ourselves more lovable. We might be conditioned by our family and society that I am this or that to feel safe and loved. This creates a persona. It is not actually who you are but is seemingly accepted by society. Sometimes, the person that I'm lying to the most is me. With this lie, I am making myself lovable to myself. Accepting who I am versus being somebody who needs to be accepted by others, is the starting point. On a side note it is ok that I was somebody who needed to be accepted by others to feel loveable, liked and part of society. This sense of belonging is something that we deeply want, it is human nature. Learning to love yourself is learning to be with all of you, and re-learning that all of you is welcome.

Revalue yourself. Look at yourself deeply. Don't try to change people, they are only messengers reflecting who you are. Revalue yourself. People around you might change, and that will confirm your new set of values. Check, recheck and revalue till it feels right.

> *CHANGE YOUR PERCEPTION OF YOURSELF*
> *AND YOU WILL AUTOMATICALLY CHANGE*
> *THE WORLD WHICH YOU LIVE IN*

WHAT KIND OF ATTENTION DO YOU PLACE ON YOUR DESIRE?

We have the power to create in our imagination and when we do so the universe responds. As a matter of fact we don't really use much of our brain capacity and everyday we learn to use less of it. Imagination is part of our brain capacity that we learn to use less of on a daily basis. Imagination is more important than science, because without imagination there is no science. Imagination enriches the world in which we live.

> *"What is now proved was once only imagined."*
>
> - William Blake

Everything was once imagined. Knowledge is a limited resource, based on research. Bring your future dream into the present, make it tangible and pleasurable. This will begin to fulfil you. You need to assume the feeling of the dream first in all its aspects, to attain the fulfilment.

> *"Imagination is the voice of daring. If there is anything godlike about God, it is that. He dared to imagine everything."*
>
> - Henry Miller

Start rising above other people's opinions. What is possible and what is not possible in your life is only known by you.

Be persistent in your dreams when others try to pull you back. Persistence is a unique quality that drives you to where you need to go. Talent won't get you there if you don't have persistence. Unsuccessful humans with talent are very common. Recognising, and building the capacity for persistence, can help you learn how to change your future.

MANIFESTATION MEDITATION

The following meditation works on your electromagnetic field. This practice is one of my favourites. I started by doing it everyday and it takes 10-15 minutes. I have found it also softens my energy. I want to invite you to find a place to sit down. Take your shoes and socks off. It's good to start with gratitude and write your goals if you have time, but you can directly start the meditation too.

The invitation is to sit in a lotus position, if you can't do a full lotus then half or gentle crossed legged sitting. Have your spine straight and comfortably upright. This is the way that you connect yourself with the universe. Allow relaxation into your body and take a few deep breaths till you feel the softening taking place. Lay your palms on your knees facing up. This is the receiving mode. Gently close your eyes and take another 3 deep slow breaths. *Inhale and exhale slowly and deeply.*

Shift your energy focus between your eyebrows, known in many Eastern cultures as the third eye or the Ajna chakra. Keep the focus there and relax into it. Keep breathing slow and deep. Just observe and be in the moment. Listen to the environment and your breath. Repeat the inhale and exhale. Keep the focus on your breathing, allowing your body to relax more and more. Just pure breathing, becoming the gatekeeper of your nose. I would like to invite you to be present here and now. Just observe the moment of now. Listen to birds, listen to your breath, listen to the sensations in the body and the quality and flavour of your mind.

The manifestation meditation works by using different breathing techniques to raise our frequency. We will be doing 4 breaths a second, which is fast breathing. See if you can begin by doing this fast breathing (known as Kapalabati breath in yoga traditions) for 30 seconds, then take a deep breath in. Do it again for another 30 seconds and after that breathe deeply in. Then return to slow, deep breathing. Hold a single pointed focus on the centre of your forehead. Now start to visualise everything that you desire. Everything that you wrote down as your dream future in Chapter 16. Imagine that it is happening now.

This is a portal that you are now entering. Keep breathing slow and deep. Look around in your imagination and see who is there and where you are now.

Use your sense of smell and feel into what is happening. Bring your palms towards your heart, one on top of the other. Ask yourself how you feel right now by sinking into the experience of this process. Feel it deeply, breathe deeply. How is your emotional landscape right now? Is it happy? Are you smiling? Do you experience laughter and joy? Or any other feeling that may arise is welcome. Just be there observing your feelings. Can you look at yourself? Let the images flow, let the emotions flow. Choose a feeling that feels good and amplify it. Let it bring you closer and closer to that reality you just conjured up. *Take another deep breath in.*

Now gently move your palms from your heart, placing them face down on your knees. Breathing slowly, feel into what it feels like to turn your palms towards yourself. In this state you will be in the attracting state. Just be, here and now. Breathe deeply a few times and settle into the experience.
When you are ready to come out of this state, start to move your shoulders gently to bring yourself back. Keep your eyes closed but begin to move your body. Move your legs, your knees, your neck. Perhaps tense your whole body, contracting all the muscles. Then release them all. Do this one more time. Rub your palms together and create heat and energy. Gently place them on your eyes and move your palms on your face across to your ears and down your neck. Open up your eyes slowly and feel into the moment. Stay present. Notice if you feel gratitude for this experience.

EXPERIMENTS

- Play nice calming music. Create a meditative sitting space. Breath deep in and out 3 times. Write your gratitude for as long as you like.
- Write 10 **SMARTF** goals for one year's time.
- Read the manifestation meditation a few times and begin to do it.
- Write down afterwards how you felt and what you experienced.

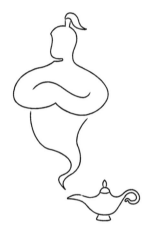

Power of Visualisation

As a kid I used to visualise every evening before I slept. Maybe you did the same? As soon as I was tucked up in bed I started to visualise that I was in a fairy forest. I was driving a train. I used to imagine all kinds of things from magical creatures or having certain superpowers. I used to play the whole day with my toys and thought that they were communicating with me. Visualising and playing. This is the nature of human children.

In society we are taught to stop dreaming and to become more realistic. For me this went so far that I almost forgot my greatest access to the universe and its intelligence. Visualising has the power to create. A human body is an ocean of motion. In other words it's an energy in motion. Energy is constantly transforming. Our thoughts are waves that are in direct communication with the universe. So when we visualise we basically form a thought that communicates with the whole universe. By having an emotion, we activate that thought process into real life. So the energy transforms and will go to the cosmos to create what it is we want. Visualising is the most marvellous, miraculous, inconceivably powerful force in the universe. With visualising, you launch the rocket of desire.

DESIRE + INTENTION + STRONG EMOTION = MANIFESTATION

You might say to yourself: 'I don't believe in this process', 'I don't want this type of life', and 'I definitely didn't visualise it!'. The good news (although this may sound hard to hear) is that you did call it in (most likely in your subconscious). Building on this good news is that you can now consciously create another desire that you resonate more with. Just observe your thought process. What you think most, is what you will get most. I will give you an example. Imagine that you feel hungry and you decide to make a sandwich. First you think of it. Then you imagine that the sandwich has tomato, basil and cheese in it. Then you act on it. You go and make it. Or just buy it. As a result you will have the sandwich and eat it. Everything can be as simple as that.

We are using visualisation all the time, for simple daily tasks but also for more complex ones. It might take more time to build a table or even a house than a sandwich but it's still the same process. We might think: 'Oh, that's so simple' and guess what? Yes it is!

If you start visualising, you build a steadfast belief that you can do things. As soon as you believe in it, you are able to take action. Sometimes our visions guide us to new discoveries.

It's important to stay open to receiving these images and to act on them. It's that simple. On the other hand, this power of visualising can be against us, motivating our fears, and activating them against you. Then we start manifesting what we are most afraid of instead of what we desire!

> *VISUALISING IS YOUR HUMAN SUPERPOWER TO CREATE. USE IT AND LET IT GUIDE YOU*

We also learned as children how to use our physical faculties. We learned how to use our eyes, ears, nose, tongue and touch - our senses. We learned how to use some of our mental faculties like memory and recall. But we were never actively taught how to use our will, our burning desire, our intuition or our gut feeling. Neither were we taught visualising or imagination processes.

Visualising is the other key muscle that needs to get stronger and requires practice. Let's do a simple practice together. Sit on a comfortable chair. Look at your hands and your body. Look at the fingers, hairs, blood veins, your skin colour and everything. Now close your eyes. Visualise what you just saw. Visualise yourself. Look at those hands once again. Now you're going to visualise your hands on the steering wheel of the car that you dream of, feeling the car seat beneath you.

Ok now, start the car, push your foot on the gas pedal and go. Feel the air as you open the window. Feel the acceleration. Look out the window and see people on the street. Really feel it. How does that feel? Does it make you want to scream? Then scream. Express how you feel. Sing a song. Remember feelings create attraction. Park your car and step out of it. Some normal questions that might come up before doing this visualisation include:

- Do I have to do this?
- Is this really going to work?

How bad do you want your desire fulfilled? You have to start the process to begin to understand and feel how it works. An example of how visualisation works: <u>don't think of a pink elephant with yellow socks on.</u>

You see. You just visualised it. Even though I told you not to think of it. Visualising is a superpower that we have and we can use it to our advantage. Many athletes visualise their next world class game. They visualise that they are winning it. It activates the same hormones and levels of excitement in their body as if they were really doing it. It is absolutely out of mind what we can do with visualising. Just do it.

WHAT IF I MANIFESTED HORRIBLE THINGS IN MY LIFE ALREADY?

Well, it is possible that this is the case. What's great is to reflect on this, and acknowledge it. The good news is that the frequency of positive thoughts is 100 times higher than the frequency of negative thoughts. So maybe it's the moment to start manifesting more of what you want! Of course, sometimes this will make you feel overwhelmed, down and low. Remember this is your guidance. You are not in the place that you want to be. So whatever the feeling is: anger, sadness, disappointment, this is a sign to move on. It is a sign that something in your life needs to dramatically change.

Sometimes it's difficult to understand what exactly needs to shift. So the best thing to do is to change the feeling first. Play some music that you like. Write down your gratitude. Talk with a good friend. Play with a newborn baby (if you can't do that in person, find a gurgling baby on youtube!). Play with your pet or go into nature and nature bathe. Take a nap. Whatever feels right. Use external sources to change your mood. I sincerely invite you to live in your happiness and excitement. In this way you can bring magic anywhere you go. A magical life that you desire, created by excitement and inner happiness.

THE ART OF LETTING GO

It's really important to relax and let things happen. When we trust we can relax. It's the moment that we can let go and make ourselves ready to receive. The more we trust, the processes we engage in will function better. To understand that, I will invite you to take a breath and look outside. Everything is working perfectly with its own imperfections. We don't have to set the sun everyday and ask birds to sing and make sure that the ocean has its own motion. All of them are working perfectly of their own accord. If I feel I have to control things, it will bring me anxiety. Maybe things fall down. If so, let them fall. See what happens now. If I hold onto things, not allowing them to fall and change, how long can I maintain that? Forever?

The art of letting go is the art of doing things effortlessly. To manifest effortlessly and to receive effortlessly too. How to be busy with what makes me happy? Let's imagine that you are a vessel, filled with whatever you need for you to be you. When you let go of the things that no longer serve you, let them fall out of the vessel. You will receive what is truly meant to be yours faster, because there is now space for it, and you are open for it.

There was a friend that I studied manifestation with. She wrote her gratitude everyday. Wrote her goals everyday and began manifesting them.

She made a vision board. She did everything that needed to be done. But after a while she called me and said *'I think something is wrong. I am still in the same place as I was 2 months ago but I have been doing the exercises daily'*. I was like: 'Wait a minute. Hold on, you have been on the other side of the matrix for thirty years! As soon as you are on the other side you expect the changes instantly?!? Give yourself a break. Maybe don't write for a while. Just breathe into it' I told her. A few months later she started to receive and of course she started to write again.

Letting go is underestimated in a society where doing is highly valued. In this case, if you let go, it means that you are useless. What you need is to actually find the balance between letting go and doing. Sometimes, just relax and make yourself ready to receive. Sometimes, work hard and make it happen. A good example of letting go is to let your wounds heal themselves. It is the same as leaving a good stew to simmer and cook after you prepare it on the fire.

To learn how to flow and let go, it is best to practice. Start with small things. Just sit in the forest or nearby nature and do nothing. Just breathe and enjoy the moment. Go fishing and just sit and observe. I know it might be difficult at first but start with baby steps. In allowing yourself to be and receive, there is nothing to run after. This is almost the opposite of what we are encouraged to do in society!

Allow yourself to dream big and trust that you came here for a bigger purpose than working in a job that doesn't fulfil you. Stop vegetating and start to shine! Allowance is an act to understand a bigger perspective. And if you don't fully get it now, let it shine onto you. You are indeed filled with this information from your birth. Abundance is your birthright and nobody can take it from you. Break the chains. Free yourself from the limits. Let the void shine through you, then everybody around you will receive the light too. Don't feel shy. The only limit is you.

EXPERIMENTS

- Play nice calming music. Create a meditative sitting space. Breath deep in and out 3 times. Write your gratitude for as long as you like.
- Write 10 **SMARTF** goals for one year's time.
- Write 'I am rich' for 5 minutes and then breathe into it.
- Name five things that you have to learn to let go of on a daily basis. How are you going to do that? Write it down.
- Go for a walk in nature and just let everything flow out of your head. Just observe and breathe. Notice the quality of your breath.

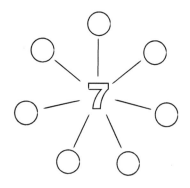

Seven Principles

I am celebrating you that you have come this far! You have made it to the final chapter! This is the last chapter of this book. I have dedicated a year to writing this book and today is the beginning of the last moon of the year. It has been a challenging year for me. How was it for you? I will share some wisdom that will help me conclude the book and bring together all of the processes I have outlined for you. These next lessons are the essence of realising your dream, achieving your life's purpose. To create and realise your own world. I call them the 7 principles. The invitation is to learn them and use them in your daily life.

1. DO IT DAILY!

All the practices that you have learned in this book are creating a new lifestyle. They are there to help you to shift your paradigms. With this information you are on a journey of integration. After completing this book, you are not finished. You learned these skills to use them in daily life. It's an ongoing journey. It's a journey to share. These new habits and lifestyles will help you grow and understand the universe and most importantly yourself better and better. It is also important to get rest sometimes, to sharpen your knives, let's say. This will help you cut faster when the time comes again. It will give you a space to see where you are and if you actually enjoy doing what you are doing. These processes are not to be hoarded, they are to be shared.

If you feel like you need to go deeper in some experiments, just do them for longer and they will take you deeper. Keep writing your gratitude, your goals and visualising them. Make new goals when you achieve the ones that you are writing now. Stay vibrant and excited. Keep doing it daily. The formula is simple:

| *ASK. STAY RECEPTIVE. DO IT AGAIN.* |

2. HAVING GOALS BIGGER THAN JUST MONEY

It's absolutely important to have goals that are based on your income and saving money. However, it's more important to find our passion, our purpose, which in turn becomes our medicine. To discover why we are here and what we can do to make this world a great place to live, we must keep dreaming and employing our imaginations. To create the world that we dream of living in, we must start seeing ourselves as artists, activists, athletes, good managers or whatever it is that instils excitement and development in us.

Since we are the creators, we have chosen to be creatures and to live this life. It's important to find out what our purpose is and dive deep into it. I recognise that this is difficult to understand and feel into. Give yourself time, keep doing different things, and take risks in your life to expand.

Remember there is nothing to lose. It's also good to see where you feel most in your zone, where you shine brightest, what you enjoy the most. Everything is a gift. Baking bread, cleaning, being a doctor, absolutely anything can bring wisdom and lessons. You have to feel in the zone. Money, as I mentioned, is a reward. A reward for your job. If you are the best, you always get the best. Regardless of your job. So let's commit to shining. Let's commit to finding our purpose and living in it. It took me 10 years to get there. I am a great host and a teacher. That's where I feel myself the best. Sharing my wisdom through teaching is where I feel most alive. I am combining these gifts and giving them back to the world. Find that reason and purpose and add it to your lifestyle and goals.

| *FIND A REASON BIGGER THAN YOURSELF.* |

3 . DISCIPLINE

Having discipline means using your willpower to commit to promises. Discipline is to give myself a command and to follow it. To realise your dream, it is important to be determined and have discipline. To have discipline means to have self control. This includes a commitment to all promises that you make, including to yourself. To let go of any excuses for not doing things, and to be motivated to do things. It means to cultivate productive pride. Again it is a muscle that you can train.

This muscle we can also apply to sleep. I would like to invite you to have discipline with your sleep by getting your sleep cycle organised. Wake up early in the morning. Get your tasks done in the early morning and you will be deadly. That's really the first and fastest step.

Determination is like having no chance to go back. To burn the boat, to stay on the island. To get the job done. Tell yourself that you are going to do it, and do it. Over time this muscle will get strong and you can manifest more and more with it.

4. TIME MANAGEMENT

A key skill in achieving success is organising your mind using a calendar, either digital or paper. I like it on paper personally. Plan the next five years and plan the next one year. Plan the next six months and plan the next month. Plan the next week and plan for tomorrow. Design the days that you would like to have.

The best method is to plan the next day every evening before sleep. Write all the tasks that need to be done. Use symbols to indicate the priority of each task. For example my indicators are a triangle and a square and a circle. So first I write everything that needs to be done. I look at them. If they are really important and urgent I will apply a triangle in front.

If they are slightly important but I can do them in the next few days, then I use a square. Normally squares are the ones that might become triangles in one or few days. Finally, there are always some tasks that might not be important to do now. They are sort of hidden. But after a few days they become square, so I give them a circle. After prioritising them I know where I have to start the day after. Planning like this helps to have a clearer mind, to have everything written out. So you can be more focused on what you need to do immediately.

Brian Tracy has this amazing small book which I recommend called *Eat That Frog*. It is about planning and how to do it. What is important is to make the most difficult task of the day the first task. That makes a lot of space in your day to achieve more and more. By eating 'your frog' first, you feel more powerful and light to do the rest. Do the most difficult and biggest task first and you will feel amazing with a lot of space to finish all the other tasks. It definitely gives you energy.

5. NEVER STOP IN THE MIDDLE AND STOP AT THE END

An important rule in life: don't stop in the middle, stop at the end. If you decide to do something, go for it. At the end you don't want to tell yourself, *'I wish I had done more'.* Live a life that you will never regret.

Obstacles are to be overcome and are to be seen as gifts, not things to make you step back and stop. You must decide when to rest but also when to push it forward. This pushing forward is the learning to continue and not give up.

Your whole life is a classroom for you to challenge yourself and learn by watching and studying. Get to know people that you admire. Learn from them. Don't stop because you feel tired. Stop doing it because you've reached a finish line. This mentality will make your road clean and soft to go further.

6. BE PROACTIVE

Ask yourself how you function when problems or opportunities arise. How do you see them and how do you work with them? Are you a reactive or proactive type of person? Be honest with yourself. A reactive person is a person that gets frustrated by a situation. They see themselves as victims most of the time. Proactive mentality sees problems as an opportunity. To find a gift in it, a lesson. To harvest good from it regardless of what took place. To express themselves as clearly as they can. The situation doesn't affect them in a way that drains self esteem but motivates them to do better. Between what you would do and what is happening, there is a space. In this space you can decide what to do if you wish. Proactive people always choose from a calm space of creation. Take a deep breath and a sip of water. Slow down to get the most out of this space.

Every time that you fail, know that you are closer to success. Be proactive in rising up.

7. LEARN NEW SKILLS

In everyday life, challenge yourself and learn new skills. Clean your tools and sharpen them. Let everything stay sharp and shiny. Let the skills inspire you to do more. Be fearless. Write your goals for 21 days to create a habit. Maybe you already have completed this during your dive into this book and practices. So the next challenge is to do it for 66 days to make it an absolute habit.

And the next... challenge yourself to do it for 90 days to create a lifestyle. Then give yourself some weeks to rest. Maybe two weeks and then start again. Learn and learn till you get inspired to create. If you have an idea, grasp it, make it real. Life is too short to think twice about it. If it feels right, go for it. I don't mean bang your head against the wall. Take baby steps. Challenge yourself. Add these new skills to your pocket for the bigger projects.

By now you know everything to realise your dream life. There will be more to learn and more chances to deepen your knowledge. This book encourages you in your exploration of the processes that can help you to create a million dollars or a sustainable hippy life. Whatever you desire.

This is a basic route to visualising and creating the life that you've always dreamed of. Today I am sitting in a villa, a few hundred metres from the ocean. I am realising my dream to live near the ocean. To surf everyday. To play music and dance. To help people achieve their dreams. To write my book and live in abundance. I have fulfilled my dream to be able to buy what I want, when I want. To see the sun shining and to be part of that shine.

I can't wait to hear your story of success. To know that one more of us has jumped out of the rat race and created a sustainable reality to inspire and aspire to. I've been sincerely inspired by so many beautiful souls who are sharing their gifts, sharing their music, their teaching, wisdom and love. Tomorrow morning I will go to the ocean and will write my gratitude to give me the power to finish this book and my goal to share it with every single one of you.

One more thing, always remember:

YES YOU CAN!

Cosmic hug and intergalactic love,

Kamran

Spiritual terms

CHAKRAS

Chakra is a Sanskrit word meaning wheel or circle. Chakras are located along the spine, which are involved between body and consciousness. They refer to seven centers of spiritual power that reside in the human astral body.

Location of each chakra:

- Root chakra located on the last spine, just above the anus.
- Sex chakra is located on our genitals.
- Power chakra is located on the belly.
- Heart chakra is located in the heart space.
- Throat chakra is located in the throat space.
- Third eye chakra is located in the middle of the eyebrows.
- Crown chakra is located on top of the head.

KUNDALINI

In tantra, Kundalini is seen as the energy of a coiled snake that sits at the base of your spine. It is connected to sexual awakening and spiritual liberation.

Resources

RECOMMENDED READINGS

McCormack, Mark - What They Don't Teach You In The Harvard Business School (1984)

Hill, Napoleon - Think and Grow Rich, Mind Power Corporation (2006)

Veary, Nana - Change We Must: My Spiritual Journey, Institute for Zen Studies (1990)

Covey. S. R. - The 7 Habits of Highly Effective People, Principles of Personal Leadership, Free Press NY (1989)

Ingram Content Group UK Ltd.
Milton Keynes UK
UKHW040618050523
421275UK00002B/72